**mental
health
series**

12

DIVISION OF THE SOCIETY OF ST. PAUL   alba house
STATEN ISLAND, N. Y. 10314

THE CHALLENGES OF LIFE

Ignace Lepp

Original title: Wagnisse des Daseins, published by Arena Verlag.

Translated by Dorothy White.

Nihil Obstat:
Daniel V. Flynn, J.C.D.
Censor Librorum

Imprimatur:
Joseph P. O'Brien, S.T.D.
Vicar General, Archdiocese of New York
May 13, 1969

Library of Congress Catalog Card Number: 75-90776

Designed, printed and bound in the U.S.A. by the Pauline Fathers and Brothers of the Society of St. Paul at Staten Island, New York as a part of their communications apostolate.

CONTENTS

Preface vii

Chapter I   The Magnificent Adventure . . . 1

Chapter II   Man: Nature's "Odd Man Out" . . 13

Chapter III   The Vocations of Men 27

Chapter IV   The Adventure of Growth 47

Chapter V   Freedom and the Process of Liberation . 59

Chapter VI   Adventure and Choice 85

Chapter VII   Availability and Readiness 101

Chapter VIII   Commitment 113

Chapter IX   The Faithful Servant 127

Chapter X   Sin and the Challenge of Life . . . 141

Chapter XI   Fear, Unrest and Anxiety 155

Chapter XII   Passion and Its Challenge 171

Chapter XIII   The Challenges of Faith 187

Chapter XIV   The Last Challenge 199

PREFACE

THE CHALLENGES OF LIFE

The world seems to grow ever more enormous and for-
bidding and men find it increasingly difficult to determine
their own place in it and feel at home. It oppresses them with
its weight of matter and its force, and they feel ever less con-
fident of having any control over it. In spite of all the power
given him by the constant progress he has made in science
and technology a man is tempted to see himself as an insignificant unit in the vast universe. Instead of ruling and
directing the world he allows himself to be ruled and directed
by it. So we have reached the appalling crisis of Humanism
characteristic of the present age, that same Humanism which
was born during the Renaissance as a direct result of man's
refusal to admit that he is subject to God. Even in the nineteenth century Nietzsche had already called upon men to
rebel against God in the name of freedom and independence.
In order that man may live God must be destroyed. Although
today men will not submit to God they are themselves dom-

inated by the material world, even if they childishly deceive themselves and claim to be its rulers. Despite the wide diffusion of culture and scientific knowledge it has become more and more difficult to find fully developed personalities, and the standardization of mankind is now considered a normal process, like the mass production of vehicles and washing machines.

"I"and "you" are giving place to the anonymous "one" and "it." Instead of human communities there are now only masses and numbers.

The existence of man considered merely as mankind in the mass is in this book described as an unreal existence. The man who declares himself content with the banalities of everyday life is incapable of preventing himself from sinking to the level of a mere cog in the wheel.

But in our opinion his descent to this level can be avoided and human abasement is not without its remedy. Let us think of this as a dialectical process whereby the age of Humanism, when man considered himself supreme, gives place to the age of nihilistic pessimism. In the new phase of development now beginning man must become aware that he is neither supreme nor a nonentity. It is enough for him to be convinced that although real life is no free gift but a task set before us, nevertheless it is possible for him to accomplish this task in spite of all obstacles. The present book would like to help people to understand this.

There are many good books full of wise reflections and fine theories about man and his existence. But today it is above all necessary to get to know men themselves with all their motives, energies, longings, desires and capabilities.

This book is not written by a theologian or a philosopher, inquiring into the eternal nature of man, but by a Christian psychologist, who concerns himself with what is temporal and tangible. His starting point is not based on speculative principles but on scientific experience. Moreover, we intend to offer the scholarly reader a book which may serve as a basis for lively discussion. Neutral objectivity is not our aim, for we would like to help all those who are seeking to understand the world and themselves, so that they may be better qualified to triumph over the false trivialities of everyday existence and to advance towards a truer and more intense life. We are utterly convinced that man's life may become admirable and worth the living only when he no longer regards the universe and himself passively, but starts actively to mold them to his will.

In several other books of mine I have, as a psychologist, concerned myself particularly with analyses. This present work is explicitly concerned with psychological synthesis. We are therefore here considering men as they are revealed to us in their total existential reality, as individuals who are at the same inseparable members of the human community. This comprehensive synthesis allows us to re-assert that man's life is neither meaningless nor absurd, but has a purpose or task to fulfill. To live a true life means accepting the human condition with its demands for creative perfection; it means not passive resignation but active acceptance.

Abstract reasoning and *a priori* deductions should be avoided. Nevertheless I am convinced that psychology will only be able to reveal man's true nature when it no longer contents itself with considering him merely from a specific point of view, for example as a sexual being or as rational being. One must take into consideration the whole of man's experience and never forget that no psychological method is capable, by itself, of discerning the whole nature of man. We shall not stray from the field of scientific knowledge even when we sometimes draw water from other sources. Many otherwise acute observers of psychological phenomena reach false conclusions because they have locked themselves within closed systems. Many exponents of depth psychology make the same mistakes in method which they discover in the earlier philosophical psychologists. The former group content themselves with observing psychopaths, and what they discover in these they believe to be common to all men. The second group, prejudiced by a materialistic attitude, refuse to take into consideration any of the spiritual, particularly the religious, experiences of mankind. They assert categorically and without any scientific proof that these experiences are unreal and the result of a pathological condition. But if we believe psychological and sociological experiences, what right have we, as scientists, to deny without proof such a generally accepted fact as spiritual or religious experience? Even if we have had no personal knowledge of this how could we lightly set aside the testimony of innumerable people of every race and age?

There was a time when rationalism enjoyed a privileged position in theology and philosophy, and even in psychology. A Christian who wished to study philosophy, or even theology, considered it his duty to ignore the tenets of his faith. He asserted that even if he were an agnostic or a heathen he would nevertheless think and write in just the same way. This method of approach resulted in a fatal cleavage between religion and the life of the mind. Neither theology nor philosophy had anything to gain from this separation.

Depth psychology is definitely a branch of natural science. But if the psychologist is a believing Christian, what right has he to reject the increase of light and knowledge which flow from divine revelation, his own religious experience and that of other men with whom he is associated?

When I first began to study depth psychology I already had some knowledge of biology, sociology and anthropology. I would never have thought it wrong to make use of this knowledge in my psychological studies. Being a Christian, have I not the same right and the same duty to make use of the light of faith? How could I judge my own life, other men and mankind in general, the universe and all material and spiritual values as an unbeliever does? If, by some intellectual process, I were to succeed in such jugglery, I should merely be demonstrating that I did not truly live my faith, and that it was like a foreign body in my psychic make-up. The Fathers of the Church and the mystics, and even such profound Christian thinkers as Augustine, Pascal and Kierkegaard, have never asserted that such an impenetrable barrier should separate faith from natural science. It should therefore be our greatest ambition to restore the broken unity between the intellect and religious faith. From our own experience we believe we may affirm that faith does not impair our natural powers of observation, but rather strengthens and illuminates them. Certainly it must not be understood as another rigid intellectual system.

* * *

Human experience, which is the subject of this book, is primarily our own personal experience, which is never merely subjective. The spiritual community, in which we are associated with many other people, permits us to presume and to believe that more or less similar experiences have been shared by innumerable other people. So I cannot claim to communicate to my readers anything 'totally new. I only wish to help them to become aware of what, for a long time, they have more or less clearly perceived, in the depths of their soul, which perhaps they have been unable to express. As a writer I feel the greatest satisfaction when readers write to me to say that I have at last expressed what they themselves have felt or thought.

I have no intention of writing anything sensational, but I nevertheless wish to startle my fellow men. Spiritual indolence undoubtedly presents the greatest danger to mankind today, a much greater danger than the atom bomb. Consequently we make no claim to an impossible neutrality: a partisan can never be neutral. Here we offer the experience of a man who from his earliest youth has taken an active part in the problems and conflicts of his time, and we invite our readers to undergo a similar experience. We are ready to guarantee that, if they do so, their lives will no longer seem to them so dull and meaningless. Our attitude will therefore be partisan, but without any intolerance.

This book is not addressed to specialists of any kind, for in my opinion they have already too many books at their disposal. Instead I would like to interest the educated layman, in all confidence, as man to man. For this reason I avoid as far as possible the use of the technical language of philosophy or psychology.

* * *

The title of this book: *The Challenges of Life,* is no casual choice. One of the main reasons for the increasing mediocrity of life today is the fact that too many people have neither the will nor the courage to embark joyfully upon the necessary challenges of life. They seek in life only repose and security, and so they give up in advance any attempt to control their own existence and submit to blind destiny. Naturally, and fortunately, there are also magnificent exceptions, men who have the courage to fly to the moon and to Venus, to climb mountain peaks, explore the depths of the earth and devote themselves to scientific research. Others bravely undertake the daily challenges of life which often requires no less courage and endurance than acts of more obvious heroism. Thanks to such people we need not despair about the future of mankind: our optimism is not naïve, for it is grounded in experience, the experience that comes to us through the knowledge amassed by many other enterprising people. And we know that there are many "simple" souls who are so daunted by the spirit of the age that, overcome by fear and anxiety, they try to refuse the challenges of life. Perhaps my book will help them to become aware of their vocation as men, and of the nobility of their human condition.

I expect many of my German readers to be scandalized when they find me showing more distrust of reason and of the mind than of passion and enthusiasm. But nevertheless I beg them to live passionately and enthusiastically. Memories of the Nazi period are still too fresh in the minds of my German friends; they mistrust any form of mysticism, or anything that seems irrational; they would like to live and act according to "pure reason" alone. Of course I understand this reaction, and I believe it is fundamentally sound. But like all reactions it goes too far. In this book I hope to show that reason and the intellect, no less than uncontrolled passion and feeling, present a danger to the individual and collective equilibrium: we must attempt a synthesis. A life without passion and love, without enthusiasm and warm-heartedness, is hardly worth living. Naturally, we are not opposed to rationalism and reason in themselves. It is only when rationalism is elevated into a system that we hold it responsible for the fearful mediocrity of most existences in the world today.

Perhaps our romantic forefathers went to the other extreme and so fell under the spell of a false mysticism. But the presence of false mysticism is no evidence against true mysticism, which demands our enthusiasm and passionate love. Our friends and readers must therefore take note that we, no less than they, are well aware of the danger of excessive emotion. However, we see in this no reason for a wholesale condemnation of human emotions and for being resigned to a cold, rational world. We shall distrust the exaggerations of emotionalism as we distrust the exaggerations of rationalism, while at the same time we shall seek to preserve the wealth of feeling and of reasoning that we find in our world.

The reader will notice that our Masters in Christian thought are above all Augustine, Pascal and Kierkegaard. Therefore, when dealing with what is called "Christian Existentialism" we shall use terms like objectivity and subjectivity. The psychologist has little inclination or opportunity to concern himself with objectivity. Man is for him never an object or a mere thing, but always a subject, a person. He is concerned with investigating not objective truth in itself but subjective, experienced truth. However, here we are not interested in mutually exclusive terms and realities but in their synthesis.

CHAPTER I

THE MAGNIFICENT ADVENTURE

In no department of life can man move with any assur-
ance — he does not work out his destiny in clear daylight.
His life is revealed and unfolded amid danger and darkness.
Whatever road he follows, whatever obligations he assumes
— all these may lead him to the goal towards which he is
straining, but he is still left with a sense of insecurity. It is
impossible to foresee all the eventual errors and wrong turn-
ings of any human undertaking. Prudence may well be
looked upon as a virtue and recommended to us as such, but
it is difficult to be prudent when we cannot foresee the future.
We read in the Gospel that Christ warned us of the prudent
rich man who made his plans for many years ahead and
ordered cellars and barns to be built so that in the future
he might enjoy all his wealth in peace. He could not foresee
that he would die the next night.

Imagine a man who loves his own ease and peace above
all else. He chooses the accounting profession, because this

seems to him the safest. He marries a girl from a good family, of excellent health, frugal, affectionate and virtuous. He mixes only with the respectable people of his own social class; he entrusts the education of his children only to schools which offer moral and social security. And to make himself all the more secure he takes out a very high insurance policy. So he thinks he knows in advance that when he is sixty-five he will retire and he also thinks that he knows what regular annuity he will receive. He believes he has excluded from his life all possible elements of risk or accident, and that he has purchased total security.

In reality this man with all his foresight has exposed himself to new dangers. It is by no means certain that even the most well-bred wife may not get bored in the accountant's home, and in the end betray him. His best clients may go bankrupt and he may be obliged to give up his practice. The devaluation of money, the nationalization of shares in which he has invested, may totally wipe out the income which he has tried to ensure for himself in his old age. The biblical Book of Job gives a good example of the precariousness of the human condition.

In earlier times there was at least a chance of relative security, and the Book of Job is describing an exceptional case. In our own storm-tossed age there is no longer any such relative security; no longer any means of avoiding the perils of life. If a man does not affront these he can only seek refuge in a neurosis. He can never know beforehand with any certainty what the choice of a friend, a profession, or even a book, or the acceptance of a chance invitation, may lead to. It may be that any of these apparently insignificant actions may prove decisive for the future orientation of our lives, and have important repercussions of the destiny of others, or indeed on the whole community.

It is even more irksome never to know with any certainty whether we are responding to our proper vocation. The possibility and risk of illusion are always present. A young man may have entered an ecclesiastical seminary or a novitiate full of enthusiasm and devotion. He is himself, as are all who know him well, absolutely convinced of his vocation. Yet after some years in the seminary or novitiate he becomes aware that this calling is not for him. He doffs his clerical habit and gets married. Is it right to declare promptly that this young man has been unfaithful to his sublime calling? It may be true, but one can never be sure. Shortly before the second World War some newly married young people, well known to me, decided that they had a vocation for the religious life and entered their respective novitiates. St. Benedict Labre tried all his life to find his true vocation and Père de Foucauld found his as a hermit in the Sahara, after being in turn an officer, an explorer, a lay brother with the Trappists and a servant with the Poor Clares in Palestine.

So it is evident that man cannot see his immediate future clearly, and that he is granted no absolute certainty about any phase of his existence. It is the same with his supernatural and eternal destiny. Certainly for thousands of years philosophers have "proved" the immortality of the human soul. The Lord's revelation and the doctrine of the Church offer us many precious indications of the nature and form of this immortality. But such objective knowledge is insufficient to satisfy us concerning a problem which is for every one of us of decisive significance. For us the existential problem is not whether the human soul is immortal and what this immortality is like, but what our own immortality will be like. As a Christian I naturally desire happiness in heaven. I know that with the help of God's grace I may achieve this, and I know also that this grace is not denied to me. But it is quite impossible for me to know beforehand whether I shall always be able to cooperate with God's grace. The records of innumerable highly favored people — from Judas Iscariot onwards — are here to deter us from having any pretensions about this. The teachings of Catholic dogma give the straight answer to our existential demands: according to the definition of the Council of Trent no one enjoys the metaphysical certainty of being in a state of grace. We can only hope for salvation.

*   *   *

From whatever point of view man considers human existence it always appears to him fraught with danger. Our destiny has to be fulfilled in time; growth is an essential law of our nature as it is an essential law of the world around us. Although saying this may displease determinists, there are no laws which permit us clearly to foresee the future development of the universe and of our common human history. All is involved in a permanent state of creation, and the act of creation remains in its innermost truth forever unpredictable. The fact that many students of natural science call the unpredictable development of the universe a mere accident is irrelevant. There is nothing in our human existence which is truly predestined. We are predestined neither to salvation nor to condemnation. No eternal decree has decided whether a man shall get married or become a monk, or whether his temporal vocation is to be a doctor, a locksmith or a teacher. Man must shape his own destiny and choose his own profession, vocation or way of life. Only a sentimental romanticism can suppose that this particular girl is predestined for that particular young man. Such a mechanical conception of Providence merely cloaks a certain indolence and cowardice, an unwillingness to undertake the risks and responsibilities of life.

The conception of adventure and risk is closely connected with that of freedom and responsibility. For animals and other natural creatures life is not, in the true sense of that word, an adventure. The flower may be plucked before the fruit is ripe; the lamb who strays from the flock and enters the wood may be devoured by the wolf. In either case we may say that this is an accident or the law of life, for neither the flower nor the lamb took a considered risk. Natural creatures, having no freedom of choice, cannot be held responsible for anything that happens to them. They will never run the risk of not fulfilling their vocation. The lamb fulfills its "vocation," that is, its destiny, just as completely whether it is devoured by the wolf in June or served up on the farmer's table in October. Of all the creatures of our world only man has a past, and a future which he has to build upon the events of the past. Although depth psychology will be able to give him a full understanding of his past, nevertheless he is still truly responsible for it. No prophet is capable of revealing the future to him, and the future does not depend on him alone. Other people, and everything that happens in the world, play their part in shaping it. Under such circumstances the risk he runs is far greater than it would be if he enjoyed absolute freedom and were himself the all powerful arbiter of his own destiny.

The risk is naturally all the greater, the more intensely a man lives, that is to say, the more freely he acts, because the springs of existential enterprise are not to be found in determinism but in freedom. But for this very reason such a man may be able to achieve great things. The coward who seeks to avoid all danger is still without total security; he encounters blind chance which, although exposing him to danger, does not give him the opportuniy of doing great things.

It may seem paradoxical but it is nevertheless true that man must not seek to avoid the hazards of life, even if he is able to do so, for if he does avoid them his vital powers will be paralyzed and he will sink helplessly into an unreal existence. Of course everyone feels a certain fear of taking risks, and while this fear is very strong in some people it is hardly noticeable in others. There is certainly no reason to feel ashamed about this, for we all try to settle down quietly and live normal lives, avoiding all danger. Neither the adventurer nor the professional revolutionary can completely escape this temptation. The famous French writer André Malraux glo-

rified the "life of danger" for many years and lived dangerously himself, before becoming De Gaulle's Minister of Culture.
Only foolish men show surprise or indignation when a former
rebel turns into a respectable citizen and, as generally happens
under the Soviet régime, seeks steady employment and takes
out a savings bank book. Even the Church of Christ, because
of the human frailty of her leaders and members, never quite
escapes the temptation to seek worldly security. She acquires
or inherits property and wealth as if our Savior had never
told us the parable of the birds of the air and the flowers of
the field. Fortunately the Lord watches over her and permits
the regular occurrence of events which put a sudden end to
false security and oblige the Church once more to embark
upon the wonderful adventure of poverty.

The modern man is particularly disinclined to undertake
the adventure of life in a joyful spirit. He is over anxious
about his own future and that of his children; he would like
to draw up all sorts of treaties to secure world peace and he
wants social legislation to protect him from the dangers of
illness and old age. Some young people, of only eighteen years
of age, choose their occupation with a view to the pension
they will receive when they are sixty. It is most necessary
that priests should very frequently explain the parable of the
over prudent rich man who built barns and cellars in order
to be able to enjoy his wealth for a long time in peace — and
never dreamt that death would so soon come knocking at
his door.

It goes without saying that we do not intend to take up a
position against social security measures, sickness benefits
and all kinds of contracts. These are all good in themselves
and marks of a progressive civilization. Only excessive confidence in these measures and the illusion that they provide
absolute security are hindrances to real living. Risks must not
be run for their own sake. Nor should everyone indiscrim-
inately be taught to make light of danger. To risk one's life
crossing a busy street simply because one is too impatient to

wait for the green light, or wilfully to dive into a raging river has nothing in common with true existential daring. It is a very different matter when a man leaps into the river to save a drowning man. The risk must therefore be weighed in relation to the relevant realities. Moreover, no true courage is shown in dissipating one's wealth by extravagance, distributing it to all and sundry, or bringing children into the world without caring what will become of them. There are therefore definite limits to be set to imprudence, and not everyone can be expected to show the same willingness to face danger, but these necessary limits must on no account be used as a pretext in order to exclude from life all elements of risk. In any case, whatever we undertake we can never be quite sure that no risk is involved. By fearing danger and fleeing from it we incur the risk of crippling our vital creative impulses, or even of being driven helplessly into a neurosis. One can easily demonstrate the fact that individuals, families, classes, peoples and nations who have lost the sense of adventure and have no higher ambition than to sit quietly and comfortably by the fireside will soon become decadent and, sooner or later, will disappear from the stage of history.

In former times the strength and greatness of the middle classes were founded on their love for an adventurous life, and these qualities enabled them to become the political and cultural leaders of their own people. Not only the middle classes of the Middle Ages and of the Renaissance but also the capitalist bourgeoisie of the nineteenth century loved to engage in big business enterprises and to play their part in all kinds of dangerous and difficult explorations. Nearly all important geographical and scientific research, as well as the colonizing and civilizing of newly discovered regions of the world, were the work of the middle classes, now considered to be conservative and behind the times.

Of course the adventurous bourgeois of former days loved money just as much as his grandchildren do today, or even more. But for him it meant not so much security and ease of life as a symbol of success and power. Adventure, far from terrifying him, had a kind of mysterious and irresistible fascination for him. However merciless his business methods may have been, he is still a more attractive figure to the psychologist than most of the middle class people of today who are often so cowardly, stay-at-home, self-indulgent and behind the times. Nowadays these people are willing to risk very little and only undertake what they consider a safe venture. They are conservative in politics and use old time-worn methods in business. Instead of trying new methods in economics, colonization and government, they cling desperately to out-of-date formulas, and stand helplessly by as their former privileges dwindle away. As a class they seem to have no future, but nevertheless among them there are many individuals who do not try to avoid the great adventure of life but cheerfully undertake it. Sociologically they may be middle class people, but psychologically they do not belong to this category.

The lot of several formerly powerful nations is equally gloomy. Let us take as a particularly poignant example the British nation which not so long ago was regarded by the whole world as bold and extremely adventurous. At that time the English were in indisputed command of all the seas, their colonies covered a fifth of the earth's surface, and British power was feared and respected everywhere. But England has grown old. Little by little she has lost her liking for dangerous enterprises. She is still proud of her former privileges and achievements and is extremely conservative in her home and foreign policies, even when these policies are directed by "Socialists." The visible result of all this transformation is the gradual disintegration of the British Empire. Already many English people have begun to understand that their country is only a relatively small island and can only survive and still be capable of greatness if she unites with other peoples. But unfortunately the majority of the British people are too much afraid of the unavoidable risks inherent in such a union and for a long while therefore set up a desperate resistance to the idea of joining the European community. And what is true of England is, with certain reservations, equally true of France and of other once great and mighty civilizations. They all chose to rest on the laurels of their famous past and to enjoy their accumulated wealth, and now they have no longer the courage to build a new future because they are afraid of the risks involved.

In the religious life also the fear of running into danger is an indication of torpidity. A truly religious person dedicates himself to the task before him without counting the cost or seeking to avoid the inevitable struggles and strains of a Christian's life in this world. He does not seek in his faith a substitute for the joys which he has renounced or an escape from the hardships of existence. Still less does he hope it may be an advantage to him in his business affairs. He disagrees with those who say that a Christian is to be envied because he knows neither fear nor spiritual unease. He knows that to be a Christian may mean persecution, renunciation, even extreme poverty or a martyr's death. He does not flee from the world and he does not scorn it or assert that it contains more evil than good and presents him with the danger of succumbing to its evil. Trusting to Christ's mercy he intends to be strong enough to resist the evil, and eventually to overcome it. The faith which enables man to enjoy the spirit of existential enterprise is certainly productive not of hypocrites but of apostles, martyrs and saints.

This religion of brave and strong men is diametrically opposed to the type of "Christianity" which claims to be a sort of insurance system against all the perils of existence. The souls of the followers of this type of Christianity are more or less unconsciously influenced by the same psychological fears which otherwise would have driven them to resort to fire and life insurances and savings banks. Miraculous medals, scapulars, indulgences and devotions to particular patron saints — all stripped of any genuinely religious feeling — are to protect them from all harm and guarantee them death in a state of grace and a safe entry into heaven. Naturally this superstitious religiosity does not inspire its devotees to fight for the coming of God's kingdom, or to be apostles or missionaries. Such people expect Christian education not to train strong and brave soldiers of Christ, but to protect young people from the temptations and dangers of life. Naturally they like to remain as much as possible in the company of other Christians, that is, of "respectable" folk.

In the age of faith, and especially during the early centuries, when Christians used to live their faith with all its attendant dangers, the manly virtues like courage, fortitude and disregard of death were especially prized. The women who became saints or martyrs showed themselves as strong as the men, and without sacrificing their natural femininity. On the contrary, the "General Insurance" religion is essentially feminine, with a great deal of pious sentimentality and many pretty devotional practices. Wherever this prevails the men either leave the Church or become effeminate.

The "Insurance" religion easily turns into a moralizing, formalizing convention which obviously is incapable of attracting the finest human natures. Moreover we know from our own experience and observation what little resistance it can offer to any grave temptation. The main objection against the Christian religion raised by Nietzsche, who had only encountered this false type of Christianity, was that it had "suppressed the sense of the challenge of life." He particularly disliked the "virtuous" Christian. He would willingly forgive all Christians "if only they were foolish enough to believe in truth, loyalty and righteousness, even if this foolishness were to cost them life itself." But instead he saw that their "virtue" consisted in the effort to prolong a life of complacent mediocrity.

Unfortunately for him, Nietzsche had no opportunity of meeting Christians like Francis of Assisi, Charles de Foucauld or even his own contemporary Léon Bloy, who was in many respects spiritually akin to him. These were people who really knew how to live and love the folly of the Cross of Christ.

Therefore, whether we amass wealth in order to ensure a secure old age, or whether we wish to make sure that our children shall enjoy a future worthy of them — whether we pursue a conservative policy with regard to class and nation or whether we put our faith in miraculous medals and candles to St. Anthony, we are always faced with a rejection of life — and that is a sign of old age and senility. Every refusal to incur the dangers inherent in life itself is a sin against human dignity.

Without the acceptance of risks there is no possibility of effective action, and the only truly active man is one who willingly braves these dangers. The so-called "intellectual" weighs and measures the pros and cons, but usually lacks the courage to proceed from theory to practice. No action can ever be completely rational. If through fear of danger we refuse to spring into the unknown we shall never become men of action. Every kind of activity requires a courage which prudent people consider to be folly. The man who acts is apparently always wrong, and the man who is content to draw cool and objective conclusions is always right.

The acceptance of existential risk forces man to emerge from his egotistic and narcissistic absorption in his own private world. The youth who dares to mount his bicycle certainly runs the risk of falling and hurting himself. But he cannot hope to get anywhere unless he risks a fall, even when the path is dangerously narrow with an abyss on either side. This metaphor well expresses our human situation. If we refuse to face danger we shall inevitably remain fixed in the humdrum monotony of daily life. If we are ready to brave all the accompanying perils of a life intensely lived we accept also the risk of falling from a height, and the unique opportunity of raising ourselves above the purely natural level of other creatures and of realizing our true vocation as men.

The joy of accepting a challenge is directly opposed to the

lust of wealth and a miserly spirit. It requires that a man shall live in expectation and in hope. How boring and how emptied of dramatic intensity our lives would be if we knew beforehand how they would develop and how they would end! If we had this foresight we should speedily and inevitably become complacent and dull-witted.

But if we courageously accept our true condition with all its perils and uncertainties we shall always remain unsatisfied and genuinely humble. The man who can never be quite sure either of his future on this earth or of his eternal salvation will have to live in and by hope. He must hope that in spite of all obstacles he will succeed in advancing along the road that leads upwards. He must hope that God will stretch out his hand to help him to rise again when he stumbles, and to rescue him when he is ensnared.

But he does not wait passively for God's help for, as we have already insisted, true adventure is always action. If he were to wait passively it would mean he had not accepted the challenge of life.

There is hardly anything more contradictory to the spirit of the Gospels than the claim to merit salvation through faith alone. However strong our faith may be, we shall always be children of hope and exposed to danger, as long as our earthly life endures. Faith also is an adventure, for we can never be absolutely sure that we believe truly and rightly.

Union with the Absolute is granted only to the man who faces all life's dangers undaunted. Only such a man will become selfless, and ready and humble enough to attempt the forward leap from our empirical world to God's presence.

CHAPTER II

MAN: NATURE'S "ODD MAN OUT"

What are we to think of this wonderful being called man who lives in the midst of the natural world and apparently disturbs its tranquil harmony? This question deserves to be answered, for of what value is our knowledge of the exterior world if we do not know what we ourselves are? Yet, whereas during the last three hundred years tremendous progress has been made in the field of natural science, our knowledge of man is hardly more complete than was that of Socrates and Diogenes. Socrates spent his time asking people questions about themselves, and died a martyr to his determination to discover the nature of man. Diogenes wandered through the busiest streets, with a lantern in his hand in broad daylight, seeking in vain a being who should correspond to his idea of a man. To neither of these philosophers was it granted to understand the mystery of man.

Aristotle, less preoccupied with the Absolute than Socrates and Diogenes, also set out to look for man. In this search he gave due importance to the similarities between men and animals. He took the definition "an animal endowed with reason" to be an adequate description of man. Man was primarily an animal, and reason was a secondary or additional quality. It certainly enabled him to rule over other animals, but did not distinguish him from them clearly enough to set him completely apart from the animal kingdom. If this rational animal were to disappear altogether, the world, according to the logic of the system, would be none the worse for losing him.

It does not seem to us that those who in our own times talk and speculate about men have made any really significant progress since Aristotle. Natural scientists and philosophers have for many centuries used so-called scientific methods in the study of mankind. Biology, history, sociology, depth psychology and experimental psychology have all had their hour of glory and imagined that they had finally solved the mystery of man. In the nineteenth century natural scientists considered him from exactly the same angle as that of Aristotle two thousand years before. For their studies of human nature they used the same methods and techniques which had proved so successful in getting to know the material world. Logically they could only see man as a relatively insignificant element in the infinite cosmos. They derided their unfortunate predecessors who had in their clumsy ignorance regarded man, this tiny particle of dust, as the center and climax of creation. However, all so-called scientific explanations of mankind have gradually been obliged to admit their failures, either by their silence or by the fact that they contradict each other so flatly.

We do not question the necessity of using scientific methods in our examination of the nature of man. He is such an exceptionally many-sided being that he can and must be made simultaneously or successively the object of the research of biologists and sociologists, psychologists and historians. All of these have already in their own sphere contributed much true and valuable information to man's sum of wisdom. We attach special importance to the contribution made by depth psychology which, unlike other sciences, observes man no longer from outside but from the innermost depths of his soul. But we must never forget that neither one department of science nor all the sciences together, can solve the riddle and penetrate the mystery of mankind.

* * *

More and more anthropologists, psychologists and philosophers recognize and admit that it is impossible to consider man merely as a unit in the immanent world order. Nowadays it is almost generally conceded that it is no part of a good scientific method to seek to understand a superior natural creature by studying only what it has in common with inferior creatures. But how can anyone seriously contest that in the general cosmic evolution man has reached a higher level than all other known creatures? Teilhard de Chardin very rightly sees in him the highest expression of the development of the *"biosphere,"* which is the animate world, and that the *"nöosphere,"* or intellectual world, begins with man and constitutes a new form of existence even though it develops in the physical world.

Several modern thinkers tend to exaggerate the difference between man and all other natural creatures. For example, Sartre considers the universe to be a closed world of its own, *en soi,* impenetrable and opaque, devoid of thought or purpose. It is simply here, without knowing why or wherefore, and without there being any more justification for its existence then for its non-existence. It lives in isolation and has no connection with anything outside it. "Uncreated, without any *raison d'être,* unrelated to any other form of life, this enclosed world is not made for eternity," writes Sartre in his famous book: *Being and Nothingness* (Citadel Press, N.Y., 1964). Side by side with this self-contained world lives man, whom Sartre calls "a being turned in on itself," a *pour soi*. He is quite transparent, and totally different from the world, which he can neither know nor in any way penetrate. Although he would like to be self-contained, *en soi,* like the world, his wish will never be gratified. Here for the first time an atheistic philosopher categorically asserts that it is impossible to fit man into the natural order, but he certainly stresses this point too much.

On the other hand, modern sciences have made a praiseworthy contribution to the general knowledge of mankind, pointing out that man is, as a creature, related to all other creatures, animate and inanimate.

The air and nourishment for our bodily needs and the light, color and sound which our souls require come to us from the world around us, as do also the images which render our intellectual activity possible. Moreover, we are also indebted to nature for our ability to exercise our most spiritual faculties, understanding and love. So it is not quite mistaken to assert that we also form part of the immanent world order. There undoubtedly exists a bond of true kinship between us and all natural creatures, even the meanest and most far removed. Our temperament and character, the peculiarities of our understanding and sensibility, are by no means unconnected with the climate, geology and geography of the land where we were born or where we have lived for many years. It is obvious that Goethe was no Greek and that Claudel, in spite of all his "universalism," is neither a Swede nor an Englishman. This dependence on the world is so close, and the conditioning of man to its forces even in the exercise of his specifically human faculties is so obvious, that many thinkers have been driven to accept determinism. More and more of our contemporaries put their trust in the old astrologers' theories, and refer to cosmic laws in their attempts to understand the destiny of man.

But the more closely we become aware of the bonds of union between man and the natural world the more clearly and significantly man stands revealed to us as an exceptional being who has been made incomparably superior to the immanent world order. We shall soon be able to determine wherein lies this superiority or pre-eminence of man with regard to all other creatures and the whole created world. For the moment it is enough to state that no revelation or interpretation, either of mankind or of the whole admirable world order, is possible if man refuses to admit the absolute superiority of man with regard to nature, and sees himself only as a part, even if the most glorious part, of the cosmic whole. The universe would then inevitably appear meaningless and repellent, devoid of all intent and purpose. This must be understood even if, as Sartre believed, human transcendence is absolute. Man lives as the ruler and king of the natural world only because he belongs to it and yet transcends it.

* * *

Mankind is not fortuitously involved with nature, like a warlike race which, in the course of its wanderings, happens to encounter a peaceful indigenous tribe which it subdues and enslaves. A world famous biologist, Pierre Lecomte du Noüy, came to the conclusion, although at that time he was still an unbeliever, that the association of mankind with nature can only be explained when we assign to man a higher purpose. Teilhard de Chardin takes the same view and many other natural scientists, believers or unbelievers, have also independently reached the same conclusion.

For countless millions of years the universe has developed and organized itself, has grown to maturity and increased its wealth. Different species arise, disappear or become transformed. Climates, geological and atmospherical conditions, the animal and vegetable kingdoms in their development and conflicts seem to be straining against resisting forces in an effort.to teach some definite goal. One has the impression that man finds himself in the midst of the great drama of a creative

evolution which has been gradually unfolding during countless ages. When it seemed that "the fullness of time" had
come, that is, when everything was ready to receive him,
there appeared, as if by miracle, a new and strange being,
man, the creation of the sixth day.

We think we can agree with Bergson's thesis, according to
which there was in the world order no fixed plan which
stipulated in advance every detail of the evolution which
led to the creation of man. Nevertheless, when we look back
into the past, we see the indisputable presence of a higher
purpose in cosmic evolution. Apparently this purpose has
directed all things. The infinitude of the universe seems to
have been created for man. However relatively small and
insignificant he may be in himself, he appears immeasurably
great and significant when we consider the long process of
development needed to prepare and create him.

But wherein lie the greatness and superiority of man in
the midst of this natural world which has begotten him and
upon which he is still dependent? Certainly this superiority
is not biological. In this respect there is no impassable gulf
between the animal and vegetable kingdoms on the one
hand and mankind on the other. The continuity of evolution
is in this sphere indisputable. In all probability man is
biologically an offshoot of the animal kingdom. He is born
into this world by the same process as all the higher mammals;
his body and most of his organs are similar to those of many
animals. It is not even so easy to prove that man represents
the peak of biological development, for in many respects he
shows a certain decline in vital power. His body is relatively
small and frail and less resistant than the bodies of animals.
He needs about twenty years to attain maturity, whereas most
of the highly developed animals need only from two to three
years. Most important of all, his instinct is extremely imperfect compared with that of apes, dogs and termites. Differ-
ing in this respect from some of their nineteenth century
colleagues who believed that man was a lineal descendant of

apes, most modern anthropologists, who profess to be "trans-formists," are inclined to believe that man is instead a sort of cousin. According to them, apes and men descend from the same remote ancestor. From our own point of view we have no objection to raise against this hypothesis, but from the apes' point of view man must seem a poor relation for whom the orang-utan ought to feel pity or contempt.

Man is therefore the head and ruler of creation only as long as he does not reduce himself to the level of a merely physical being. So we see that there must be something in him which is different from mere physical existence and superior to it. This "something" which is man's true dis-tinguishing mark, can only be spirit. We do not yet know much about man's earlier preparatory life in the natural world, but from our point of view this ignorance is relatively unimportant. Whether our biological origins are to be found in apes, or in a great uncle of the ape family, or whether (as a French anthropologist more or less seriously tried to dem-onstrate some years ago) in the tortoise, or whether the Creator fashioned our bodies directly out of mere matter — these are undoubtedly very interesting questions, although the answers which man is capable of finding for himself can tell us very little about the human species. These genetic characteristics tell us nothing about man's immanence or tran-scendence with regard to nature. Palaeontologists have dis-covered several skulls which hardly enable them to say whether they belonged to men in the first stage of their devel-opment as men, or whether they belong to the highest stage of his evolution as an animal. Those who deny human tran-scendence had no cause for rejoicing when they thought they had discovered the proof that there was a linear continuity be-tween animals and men, and equally mistaken are many believers who see in these discoveries a danger to their Christian faith.

Man appears in world history at the same time as there appear the first signs of the presence of a spiritual power.

According to the Christian conception of the universe it is by no means impossible that the gift of the spirit was granted to a creature less biologically perfect than many others. In any case it is beyond a doubt that the appearance of the spirit in the history of the universe was something totally new. The predominance of determinism is therefore finally ended, and the era of invention and of creative action is beginning. This does not mean that the universe has ceased to develop. On the contrary, its growth is more intensive than ever before, but now it finds its fulfillment above all in the spiritual realm, for biological development seems to have reached its end. The appearance of the soul introduced a completely new element into the sphere of vital growth. The vital impulses are no longer subject to immanent, mechanical laws, but are guided and checked by another dynamism whose power is infinitely superior and which we dare to call a spiritual force.

We are not particularly impressed by apparent agreements between the Christian revelation and the discoveries of natural science today. A *rapprochement* of this kind nearly always proves to be deceptive, and at the beginning of this century played evil tricks on many Christian thinkers. We would however point out to our readers that the religious point of view, which we have already indicated, does not conflict with the results of scientific investigation. Present day natural science considers evolution, or the transition from one kind of being to another, to be a firmly established fact. As Teilhard de Chardin says: "Transformation no longer presents any problem: it has been finally accepted. In order to shape our conviction of the truth of biogenesis it would be necessary to uproot the tree of life and undermine the so-called structure of the world." This opinion is however in no way opposed to the Biblical revelation which speaks of our immediate creation by the hand of God. The appearance of contradiction is there only because we often forget that revelation and natural science describe two aspects of truth.

Scientists describe the natural life of the universe and,

as we have already said, it is quite obvious that man in his natural state was developed from an animal. Revelation, on the other hand, is concerned with the transcendental order and it is certain that the transcendent principle of man, his spirit, is of no natural origin. When the difference between these two orders is admitted, then we must not be disconcerted to find men who call themselves palaeontologists, or depth psychologists, or believing Christians, all equally convinced both of the evolution of species and of God's direct creative work — and this without any inner conflict in their reasoning process.

* * *

How is it that so many eminent natural scientists and philosophers have made such grave blunders with regard to man's true nature? The methodological fault of all rationalists who wish to unveil the mystery of man may be attributed to their habit of trying to understand the higher forms of nature by studying those which are inferior, that is, they try to understand men by concentrating on what they share in common with animals. If science had begun with the study of spiritual reality and afterwards proceeded by gradual stages to a study of more and more primitive creatures, our conception of the universe would most probably be very different from what it is today. But the historical facts are that the first western thinkers, mathematicians and physicists, were primarily interested in the most external, material and objective realities.

When later on they began to observe more sublime and complex realities they naturally continued to use the method which had been so successful in exploring the world of matter, and so they could not resist the temptation to try to reduce higher forms of life as far as possible to the dimensions of lower forms. So began the levelling process which logically had to result in the modern philosophies of the absurd.

In reality all creatures find their justification and explanation in the light of the function which they fulfill and by which they are dominated. A fragmented universe consisting of creatures all separate from one another can only be an absurd misconception. Matter is created for life, life for the spirit, the spirit for God — that is what, with St. Paul, we must believe.

Certainly, in order to know about men we must find out all we can about his similarity to animals, plants and the whole cosmic order which he serves and which serves him, and also his relationship to these. But in order to discover the true nature of man we must also, and above all, consider him in his relations with what is higher than himself, that is, with God. Consequently an honest scientist must confess that however great and valuable the contribution made by natural science to our knowledge of man — and indeed they have contributed a great deal — nevertheless man in his total reality cannot be merely the object of scientific research. There is present in man some essential element which is specifically human, which cannot be the object of any scientific investigation, and which belongs entirely to the realm of mystery.

In saying this we do not mean of course that there can be no scientific anthropology. Like the understanding of any other mystery an understanding of mankind can only be complete when that other sphere of knowledge, concerned mainly with what is mysterious, is called in to our assistance. Human life indeed presents a biological, psychological and sociological problem but it is also a religious mystery. Every problem has a solution, but for a mystery there can only be an illumination. The Christian anthropologist therefore disdains no natural source of knowledge and fears no danger to his faith from scientific truth, but he is capable of interpreting and deepening his natural knowledge by drawing from other sources.

Human life would be a hell without an exit if men and the world in which they live were merely immanent, if there were nothing else more remote and sublime, nothing more profound and mysterious. On the existential plane man and God are two correlative conceptions. The man who rejects God is no longer a man but only a creature *pour soi,* a thing without density or stability, without a *raison d'être,* not knowing whence he comes, whither he goes or even what he is. Sartre has understood this with extraordinary clarity, and his disbelief in this absurdity is indisputably much more logical than other kinds of atheism which deny the existence of God and yet seek to assign a purpose to life.

We see in God not the logical conclusion of a rational inquiry but the explanation of life's deepest mystery. When we carefully examine human existence, activity and thought, we cannot help coming up against the highest reality of all, God. Philosophers who speak of an inborn sense of God are not entirely mistaken, when they grasp the problem in its entirety.

In any case we can only learn about ourselves and our relationship to the world around us when we recognize that we have been made in the image of God.

If we were to be content with considering men merely as individuals, as isolated beings, we should be abandoning the solid plane of reality and find ourselves left with a worthless abstract conception. Real living men are by their very nature social animals. There is hardly any serious problem which they do not share with their brother men. Every time a man isolates himself and claims to fulfill his own destiny in arrogant self-sufficiency he fails and becomes less than human.

The social nature of man is so obvious that Aristotle, who was the first to define him as an "animal endowed with reason," completed the definition by adding that he was "made for society." The old philosopher saw that this "sociability" was as characteristic of man as his "reasonability." Indeed the isolated man enjoys no true life. Everywhere men live in societies, generally in societies larger than the family group. The evolutionary socialists of the nineteenth century had believed that in a primitive state men lived in mass formation, without any awareness of their individuality or of that of others. But all modern ethnologists agree that this sort of gregarious life is not to be seen in any of the most primitive races which still survive here and there, and students of prehistoric times have found no trace of such hordes of men in the most remote past. Everywhere man seems to have been aware of himself as an individual living in a more or less close relationship, according to his degree of civilization, with other men whose individualities he recognized.

Sociologists of the school of Emile Durkheim were so fascinated by this conception of the social nature of man that they believed it was proved that man was merely a product of society. Only society was a true ontological reality and created men in its own image. Even God himself was, according to them, merely an imaginary personification of this society. It is easy to recognize in this thesis the marks of Hegel's theory, according to which the Universal alone has ontological reality and stability. Hegel had a similar influence also on the Marxist conception of man: true reality was possessed only by the proletariat, the party and the state. The individual was only a small part in all this and owed all his reality and value to society as a whole, to which he belonged and which he served. The existentialism of Heidegger and Sartre, on the contrary, was almost exclusively concerned with the inner mystery and incommunicability of the individual, and therefore was sternly condemned by Marxists.

Naturally we do not agree with these exaggerated ideas of the sociologists and Marxists. But we must admit that a man exists in this world only in association with other men and because of other men, just as all other men are equally dependent upon him. In human society, however, in which human solidarity is so clearly emphasized, man remains an autonomous person who has to fulfill his own vocation.

Psychologists and philosophers, who seek to understand not only an indeterminate eternal Essence but the nature of man's actual existence, assert that man must always be considered as preconditioned by circumstances. This concept of his conditioning is very important when we wish to discover the possibilities and limitations of freedom, vocation and occupation.

A first conditioning takes place even before a man is born; he inherits it with his life and it becomes identified with him. If we had been born in Marseilles or Munich we should be from the start conditioned as a Provençal or a Bavarian.

This peculiarity is apparent in some of our ways of speaking and of reacting, as well as our temperament and character. Similarly, it is bound up with our original social condition, our religion and degree of culture; the son of a ragpicker, born and reared in a wretched home, can only with great difficulty free himself from this early conditioning even if his gifts or good fortune allow him to become a statesman, a great actor or a tycoon.

This pre-conditioning leads to other sorts of conditioning of which man is unaware, whether he suffers it or transforms it, and all these fuse together to form his personality. The calling he chooses, the woman he marries, the children he begets and the friends he makes all become part of his total personality, in the same way as the period and civilization in which he lives and the religion and culture which nourish his spiritual life. If a man were to cut himself free from any kind of circumstantial conditioning he would no longer have any kind of existence, he would be merely a logical abstraction, an indeterminate essence.

But we do not hold with those doctrinaire phenomenologists who believe that man is merely the result of successive dissolving circumstances. In our opinion man is superior to any possible situation in which he may become involved. It is he who gives meaning to these — not they who give meaning to him. When we describe man as a "conditioned" being we mean that he is here present in a physical body and that it is in this only that he is conditioned.

CHAPTER III

THE VOCATIONS OF MEN

In the general scheme of the universe what place and what role are assigned to man, who is at the same time part of nature and superior to it?

Our forebears thought that man had only to live out his predestined fate, which for every man had been fixed for all eternity and was as unavoidable as sunrise in the morning or sunset at close of day. So there was no possibility of escaping it or altering it in any way. All a man had was a certain possibility, offered him by astrologists and prophets, of finding out what his particular destiny was to be. This complete subordination of human existence to a universal fatalism and determinism meant that life loomed as a tragedy, with no visible means of exit. This very absence of all consolation and hope was what attracted Nietzsche so much in the Greek conception of man. On the other hand rationalists, whether materialists or idealists, absolutely refuse to concede that there is anything tragic or mysterious in human life. For them it is only a question of pressing forward in the direction indicated by reason. Their ideal is, as far as lies within their power, to rationalize the world and their own existence. They are willing to consider themselves as a mere link in a chain which has neither end nor beginning. But such total rationalization can only be admitted on the assumption that there is no life beyond the grave and no mystery. Instead of mystery there is only the "unknown," and it is permissible to hope that one day the unknown will be fully revealed. In our opinion this rationalistic thesis can only be defended on the plane of pure theory. The Marxists, who after the Russian revolution of 1917 tried to live by this theory, soon had to admit that the so-called rational illumination can shed no true light on the alarming questions which confront every man who has reached a certain stage of spiritual maturity: Who am I? Why am I here? Where am I going? A man can indeed avoid these questions for a certain time, but one day he must find a satisfactory answer to them.

The prominent atheist thinkers of our own times — Sartre, Camus, Malraux — agree with us in discarding this rationalistic view of mankind, because they also find it too superficial and inadequate to express the more profound realities. They have discovered the fundamentally tragic nature of existence. They believe, with the ancient Greeks, that this tragedy is due to fate and predestination. Man moves here and there, is aroused to enthusiasm, undertakes great things, destroys and rebuilds, stirs up wars and revolutions — but in reality achieves nothing and remains forever immured in his own solitude. We are all merely "unburied dead" and in spite of all we succeed in doing we shall never be able to escape from our own nothingness. At best Malraux sees but the possibility of rebellion, but even rebellion is unavoidably doomed to failure.

This does not mean that Sartre and other atheistic existentialists doubt man's freedom of choice. As we shall point out in a later chapter, they are indeed rather inclined to exaggerate this freedom. But freedom as Sartre understands it in no way diminishes the inevitability of destiny: it is rather an integral part of it. It is yet another fetter for man: he is sentenced to freedom just as he is sentenced or predestined to be a thief or a paederast. Whether a man reads Heidegger or Sartre or the innumerable novels and plays inspired by their philosophy, in every case he is aware of the same odor of despair and death.

Certainly there are many men who never trouble to ask themselves any questions about the meaning of life. They are what they are, hardly aware of their debt to a historical or cultural background, or of being conditioned by their circumstances. They are content to behave and act as others around them customarily do.

They work, eat, drink, marry and beget their kind. They are, and wish to be, "like all the others." They are submerged in their daily round and satisfied with it. No struggle, no yearning or ambition disturbs their slumber. It is not only among the primitive tribes of Africa or in the lowest state of our own society that we find such people — they exist everywhere, in all social classes, even among the highly educated. By far the greatest majority are found in decadent societies. By their unreal kind of life they belie their human nature, for in practice they refuse to acknowledge and to accept human transcendence: they are merely things among other things.

A true man denies the inevitability of failure. He knows that he has enormous creative power at his disposal. Man is in reality neither an animal endowed with reason nor a merely economic unit. From the point of view of dynamic existentialism, which we have made our own, there is only one description capable of expressing the resources and capabilities of man. He is "the creature with a vocation." In spite of preconceived notions — which are moreover to some extent justified in so far as they contradict the over hasty conclusions of a naïve and superficial finalism — the indisputable achievements of natural history and science appear to confirm the hypothesis that all the natural creatures of our universe are striving to reach a certain end, although it is not always quite clear what the final end of every creature is to be. Natural creatures achieve their purpose as it were mechanically, by means of an immanent automatism. On the contrary, men must listen to the cry in their innermost souls which orders them to take the direction of their lives into their own hands. A man must try to discover his Creator's special intention with regard to himself, and he must direct his life according to this purpose.

Certainly man does not have to create himself out of nothing. In every phase of his existence he finds himself in a situation which impels him to press forward and shape his life himself. In order to be able to fulfill this vocation it is his duty to exploit all the possibilities of every given situation. He must not fail to use either his physical powers or his spiritual gifts, for nothing that God has given him is superfluous for the fulfillment of his wonderful human destiny. He must certainly find time for thought, if he is to perfect himself as man, because thought alone is capable of giving him a true understanding of himself, of others, of the universe and of God. Any kind of action too is, to say the least, as indispensable as thought because through action man exercises his power over the world, takes possession of it and assigns to it the meaning God intended for it.[1]

We do not put forward our vocation as the only reality, in opposition to destiny considered as error or illusion. Undoubtedly the strong influence of biological and sociological determinism still weighs heavily upon man's life. Countless people are so much affected by this burden of determinism that the role of personal vocation is reduced to a minimum. Even the most spiritually minded and most highly educated

---

1. This difference between thought and action is not found in mystical meditation, in which the initiated find the highest form of activity.

men never quite get rid of this determinism which may be thought of as a belief in blind destiny. It is therefore impossible for us to agree to Sartre's point of view, according to which man is absolutely free and consequently is himself his own vocation — in so far as it is possible to speak of any of Sartre's people having a vocation at all. Moreover, we have already seen that Sartre's freedom is itself a kind of doom.

But, however heavily destiny seems to weigh upon man's life, we will not give way to pessimism. Through our own personal experience, as also through our sharing in the experience of others, we know that human destiny is not an implacable fate and that man can overcome determinism. The man who refuses to see the universe as a hellish solitude, the man who discovers his own transcendence, transforms what was originally mere fatality into a means by which he can construct his own personal vocation.

* * *

Everyone has two vocations. The first of these summons him to ascertain the purpose of his life while the second requires him to make use of all the means at his disposal in order to achieve this purpose. We call the former a transcendental and the latter a temporal vocation. The transcendental vocation is common to all men. As he is a spiritual being man does not belong wholly to nature. Being made in God's image he is in a certain sense God's representative in this world. But, as he is not only spiritual but also truly akin to all the creatures of this empirical world, this likeness to God is never perfect in any man. At the start of his life he enjoys only the promise of perfection; gradually, as he overcomes obstacles and conquers difficulties, his likeness to God becomes more perfect. So man's fundamental vocation is to become like God. This call comes to all men and no one can fulfill his purpose as a man unless he responds affirmatively to this calling.

We must not consider this transcendental vocation as if it were something optional or of secondary importance, something additional, over and above a man's natural vocation. In actual fact men do not have to choose between two directions, one towards a natural end and the other towards the fulfillment of a supernatural purpose. No one can without detriment to himself choose an exclusively earthly vocation, which may be fulfilled by the practice of the natural virtues only. When we describe the other as a transcendental vocation we do not mean that it is the costly and glorious privilege of specially chosen people, of whom it is said: they have a special vocation. In fact every man has a special vocation, and no other kind exists. The special transcendental vocation is the same for all.

Man must never forget that he is only man by virtue of his spiritual nature and that this spiritual nature consists chiefly in responding to God's call and God's expectations. Men seek an ever more perfect likeness with the One in whose image they are made. This is so obvious that even such a totally unbelieving philosopher as Jean Paul Sartre understands it. Man, writes Sartre, is a creature who intends to be God. He becomes aware of God first in his heart, and so he conceives this primary purpose of becoming God. Being a man means trying to be like God; man's fundamental desire is to become God. But for Sartre, who from the start rejects the religious experience of mankind, this fundamental desire is futile and impossible to satisfy, and therefore human existence is merely a meaningless agitation which can only result in failure.

But we must ask ourselves the question: what right have we, as seekers after the truth, to reject the increase of understanding which can come from Christian revelation and the religious experience of innumerable people? Certainly, we shall never succeed in becoming God, or in losing ourselves in God. But our likeness to God can become valid enough to enable a mystic to speak of life in God, of the substitution of

Christ's heart for his own, and so on. To use Christian ter-
minology: neither before nor after original sin, nor even since
our Redemption have we found ourselves in the so-called
"state of nature." The notion of a pure natural state is merely
a recent theological theory, useful perhaps on the speculative
plane but dangerous when used on the existential plane.
Just as the God of the philosophers is no God of nature, so
man, made in God's image, cannot be called to a purely natural end. Man may through sin be temporarily removed from
God, but he is still subject to him and his vocation is to be
with him. What we call a transcendental vocation is the con-
junction of the divine call with the free human response to it.
Men may fail to respond to this calling and fail also to discover their own natural vocations.

Considered superficially, this lack of a natural vocation
may seem indicative of man's limitations. All other creatures
in the world have only to be what they are, in order to achieve
their final purpose, whereas man can only achieve his final
purpose by rising above himself or, as the mystics and existentialists say, by annihilating himself. And it is here that man's
true greatness lies! He alone strains ever forward and upward
and renounces indolent ease, for it is his nature to be a seeker
after God.

*　　*　　*

The ways of fulfilling men's vocations are as diverse as
the men themselves. Everyone must choose the temporal calling which is most suitable for his personal life. The temporal
vocation chosen by St. Anthony in order to fulfill his transcendental vocation was to withdraw into the desert in order
to pass his life in penitence and prayer. St. Simeon lived for
many years on the top of a high pillar. St. Francis and St.
Clare of Assisi distributed their goods among the poor and
proved to the world that life can be beautiful and happy even
in poverty. St. Louis was an excellent king of France and

St. Anna Maria Taigi devoted herself wholly to her drunkard of a husband and her numerous children. The Jocist, the "activist" of the Young Workers' Movement, works by day in a factory, that in so doing he is of use to many of his unknown brethren. In the evening he accompanies the other young people of the district to the cinema, the local inn or in dance, in imitation of Jesus who was present at the wedding at Cana, and in order to bear witness to him everywhere. The temporal vocation of some is to get married, of others to renounce the joys of family life. All these apparently diverging ways lead to the same Father's house. The best way for a man is the way which allows him to live most fully, which obliges him to be most generous, magnanimous and self-denying. We may say that, generally speaking, the more conducive a vocation is to the good of all, the more glorious it is. This, however, does not mean that the same vocation is necessarily the most glorious for every individual. The boy whose parents want him to become a monk, and who instead decides to be an artisan, must not be said to have betrayed his nobler vocation. He might have been a very mediocre monk, and he may be and excellent artisan. All this seems very clear and simple in theory but in real life frequently appears very complicated and confused.

Our attitude to our transcendental calling — whether we have learnt of it through our parents or teachers or through a direct intervention on God's part — is comparatively simple: we either accept it or reject it. It may happen, moreover, that a man remains bravely faithful to his transcendental vocation without knowing exactly what it really is. This happens to all people of good will and great honesty who for various reasons have not found the true God — only the extreme Jansenists have condemned these to the fires of hell. Everyone who conquers the wastefulness and dissipation of ordinary daily life and becomes conscious of his innermost self, which means the depth of his metaphysical being, discovers in his heart a passionate need of greatness, a compulsive urge to

rise above himself. Therein lies the root of man's will for
power about which Nietzsche has spoken, many times much
to the point but more frequently with exaggerated emphasis.
The further man progresses in the way of true life, the
stronger will grow his will for power. It is the inner expression
of a spiritual impulse which comes from God and is intended
to raise man beyond this life and the living world around him.
The man who has not discovered the root of this will for
power which he feels within himself follows false gods and
sinks more or less consciously into idolatry. He has become
fully aware of his intense desire for greatness and therefore
he wants to win power: so he becomes a statesman or a revolutionary. But it frequently happens that in his fever for
action he can no longer hear his inner voice, and so lets himself be carried away by the powerful impulse that spurs him
on. Then the danger arises that he will become one of those
de-humanized idealists, many of whom have come to the fore
in recent wars and revolutions. If, however, the man of action
does not cut himself off from his inner life then there is
hope—history and everyday life bear witness to this—that
one day he will understand that his thirst for greatness can
never be appeased by a purely temporal victory. The more a
man conquers and dominates, the more hungry and empty
he will feel. Then he will ask himself whether this natural
thirst, which no earthly source can satisfy, may perhaps have
been given him so that he may become aware of another kind
of thirst, so that he may long to drink from a source that is
not of this world.

Some will be drawn out of the humdrum monotony of
their lives by art, the love of nature or a sentimental desire
for revolutionary action. For a certain time this will give them
the sensation of true fulfillment, and even of intoxication.
However, if they are brave enough fully to express this inner
urge, they will discover that they have been swimming in
some inland lake, bigger or smaller as it may be, but not in
the open sea. To reach the ocean, that is, to live a truly

spiritual life, they must break through all existing barriers and abandon themselves to the ocean tides. On the other hand we must point out that those who have ventured out into the lake may be, even without knowing it themselves, quite ready to swim in the open sea. This means that a person who has overcome his self-centeredness and devoted himself to a cause greater than himself — even if this cause is merely human and objectively bad or misguided — is nearer to God than another man who may know God by name but will take no risks and consoles himself with the thought that he does no harm to anybody. The idolater too has heard the call, but too indistinctly to recognize his true vocation as man. Nevertheless he decides to try to discover what it is. We feel quite sure that it is better to set out on our way, even if it is in the wrong direction, than to stay where we are with the excuse that we do not know exactly which the right way is. And of course very few men will find the right way as soon as they set out. Sören Kierkegaard distinguishes three phases, all of which have to be passed through by the man who seeks his true vocation, and he calls these phases aesthetic, ethical and religious.

The man who is sensitive to beauty, who is enthralled by music, painting or nature, has certainly already succeeded in breaking the humdrum monotony of everyday life. This is even more true of the man who has reached the ethical phase, who truly and actually loves goodness, modesty and honesty and is capable of selflessness, even of sacrificing himself to a cause which he considers good. Normally the love of beauty should open the door to the religious way. Only when a man reaches this last stage, which brings him into direct contact with God, will he have realized his true transcendental calling. Sad to say, this normal process does not always take place. It frequently happens that a person is completely satisfied with the discovery of beauty or ethical goodness and enjoys the pleasure he finds therein in an egoistical way. Then we have the aesthete, or the respectable "do-gooder," the gentleman, and not one of these will be able to realize more than a truncated version of his vocation. The beauty of art or of nature, or an ethical code, may therefore instead of leading us to the religious phase become umbrellas which prevent us from looking higher, because they make us believe that we have reached the summit while in fact we are still on the mountain slopes. The aesthete and the gentleman are often impervious to true spiritual values because they are satisfied with what they have achieved.

When passing from the aesthetic to the ethical and from the ethical to the religious it is not necessary to deny or to discard the values we have discovered in the earlier phases. On the contrary, the higher phase has to take over and integrate everything of value in the preceding phases. We learn this above all from the experience of famous musicians, painters, poets, philosophers and men of action who were also deeply religious. Would anyone, in full knowledge of the facts, dare to say that Péguy became a poorer poet, or Bergson a poorer philosopher, after his conversion?

Is it absolutely necessary, for everyone who wishes to reach the religious stage of his existence and so to discover his true transcendental vocation, to pass through the aesthetic and ethical stage?

The histories of conversions and the lives of many saints seem to prove that the religious stage may be reached directly from the aesthetic stage or even from the ethical stage alone. When the French novelist Huysmans was persuaded by the beauty of Christian worship to give Christ the most important place in his life he was still, to all appearances, not a virtuous man. On the other hand, a virtuous man may often be totally insensitive to aesthetic pleasure, without this defect preventing him from becoming a true believing Christian or even a saint. It is true however that the man who begins his religious life with a certain equipment of human values — like the man who is sensitive to beauty and accustomed to living virtuously — may experience a fulfillment which even the saints themselves, if poorly endowed by nature, cannot know. The religious man who is rich in moral virtues but poor in aesthetic appreciation is often prone to a Pharisaic rigidity and takes pleasure in stern and arid apologetics. It is hard for him to understand that the beauty of this world can have such a powerful fascination over many other men. On the other hand, the examples of men like the poets Baudelaire and Verlaine and many other artists prove that the religious life of famous aesthetes who abide by no moral principles is very fragile and often full of illusion. Both Gide and Cocteau, who for a time were drawing nearer to Catholicism, later on spoke of merely "literary conversions," because their lack of moral perseverance made it impossible for them to attain a true religious state.

Our transcendental vocation is fulfilled not in fixed eternity but in time, and therefore in and through the actual conditions of our existence. All the advantages which we can add to our natural state perfect our temporal vocation, without making it impossible for us to fulfill the eternal vocation which is common to all men.

* * *

It is often difficult even for an intellectually mature and highly developed human person to discover his true temporal vocation. We are never quite sure either that we have discovered it or that we are following it. As we have already frequently pointed out, the fulfillment of our natural vocation is the condition for the fulfillment of our transcendental vocation. For this reason many saints thought they could have no certain knowledge of their own salvation. Francis of Assisi trembled for his own soul even when the whole world already revered him as a great saint. Kierkegaard also wanted men to understand that there was only ever one true Christian, Christ himself, for all others are only seekers after Christ. So it comes about that, despite the opinion of Nietzsche, life appears just as much a tragic drama to the Christian as to the unbeliever. Indeed, although we profess the Christian hope, this hope is by no means easy to come by and is no superficial optimism.

In order to discover his temporal vocation and to realize it — and by so doing to lay the foundations of his eternal vocation — man must first of all become as fully aware as possible of the actual conditions in which he lives. If many of our contemporaries vegetate in the unreal monotony of daily life, it is because rationalism, which has more or less directly moulded them, has completely misunderstood the true nature of man. Rationalists consider and handle man on the theoretical assumption that he is sound and well balanced, and that he instinctively desires happiness and harmony. Consequently, the realization of a vocation appears to them almost exclusively dependent on external circumstances, institutions, laws and political-social conditions, and man places all his hopes in their transformation.

But in reality man is an imperfect and paradoxical creature. Even if he could create perfect institutions, laws and constitutions, we should still never be quite sure that he could or would wish to attain happiness. This can be explained by the fact that the individual's notion of happiness is never rational: everyone longs not for a common ideal of well-being but for his own individual happiness, and finds his true happiness more in the accomplishing than in the accomplishment of his destiny.

Modern psychopathology is an important element of scientific anthropology. For example, we now know for certain that there is no fundamental difference between the neurotic and the "normal" person, the truth being simply that certain features characteristic of all men are in the former group accentuated or distorted. Already, long before Freud and Jung, Augustine, Pascal and Kierkegaard were aware that man is by his very nature a two-fold creation. Groping in twilight, if not in total darkness, he has to discern and follow his vocation. In him the gravest contradictions, which abstract logic declares to be totally irreconcilable, are existentially reconciled. The same man who in all sincerity professes brotherly love for all men shudders with hatred of his neighbor. Dostoyevsky, with his shrewd understanding of men's souls, showed that a man can at the same time love and hate the same person. The greatest magnanimity is often found in a man's heart together with the most savage egotism. We know politicians of the Left who are real tyrants in their private lives, and conservatives whose political and economic — or even moral and religious — liberalism astounds us. That young girl whose purity we admire may not herself know how much impurity is concealed in her heart and mind. The Bible tells us that Moses was the mildest of men, and yet this same Moses could be extremely fierce and violent, even capable of cruelty. In order that man may fulfill his vocation, despite this two-fold nature and its inherent contradictions, he must discover in himself a superior principle of unity. If he were to accept his double nature as a final and unalterable condition he would, because of the constant strain of these contradictory tendencies, become disintegrated and submit helplessly to the humdrum monotony of daily life. The temporal, natural vocation has, in practice, to play the role of this unifying principle.

The knowledge of what we are and, most of all, of what we may become, is indispensable for the discovery of our natural vocations. We can fail to fulfill our vocation in two ways: first of all, by not taking enough pains to discover it, and secondly by not having the courage to follow it. The conditions of our life today are not favorable to man's self discovery. A more profound self-knowledge can indeed only be attained in silence and recollection, for only then can the talents and gifts with which our Creator has enriched our nature be revealed. We do not deny that there may be vocations which require the sacrifice of our natural gifts. However unwilling we may be to admit this, there were indeed some saints who renounced not only their material but also their spiritual endowments in the certainty that in so doing they were obeying the will of God. In order however to justify that sort of sacrifice it is necessary that God should declare his demand just as clearly as he did to Abraham when he required the sacrifice of his son Isaac, the "heir of the promise." In any case such demands are exceptional. For the majority of men — in the framework of what we may call the normal economy of divine providence — the natural gifts and talents are seen to be most useful signposts in dictating the road which they are to follow, in order to discover and answer their true calling.

*   *   *

First of all there are negative indications: if a man has no ear for music he must not decide to be a conductor. But the positive indications always require more courage: it is not at all certain that the youth with a ready tongue should become a lawyer or a politician. But when a man has chosen the way which quite objectively he considers most suitable for him to follow, he still needs great courage to set out upon it, for the way uphill is often steep.

Although there is no infallible sign by which a man can be sure of having chosen the right way, nevertheless the individual who has found his own generally enjoys a feeling of joy and peace which permits him to presume that his choice is not entirely mistaken. We deliberately speak of joy and not of pleasure because it can be felt in the midst of hardships, grief and suffering, whereas pleasure is incompatible with these. If today there are so many joyless people around it is most probably because they have become more or less aware either that they have not found their right road or that for some reason or other they have not followed it. Modern life is too agitated to offer the majority of men the peace and tranquillity they need to get to know themselves and to recognize the vocation whose sign is impressed upon their innermost souls. The obstacles to the discovery and fulfillment of a man's vocation are therefore set up not only by his individual nature but also by the society in which he lives. The de-personalization and excessive mechanization of life are the reasons why most men find it so hard to discover their true vocation or to follow it when found. If all we do for the betterment of human life is to be effective, we must work at the same time in both spheres of activity, the individual and the social; we must endeavor to transform both the individual and the society in which he lives.

It happens but rarely that failure to fulfill his natural vocation prevents a man from following that vocation which is transcendental. The youth who, to all appearances, is drawn by his own personal qualities and by the call of grace towards the priesthood, but has married because he has not heeded the voice that speaks in his innermost soul or perhaps because he has not had the courage to face the sacrifices inseparable from priestly vows, is not thereby totally prevented from contributing to the setting up of God's kingdom. He may, for example, turn his married state into a true vocation, and God will undoubtedly never deny him his help, for jealousy of that sort is not a characteristic of the God we know from the Gospels. Probably this young man may during his married life experience some doubts and difficulties which he might have been spared if he had become a priest, but he will still be able to fulfill the transcendental vocation in which all men share. This is all the more true of temporal vocations which imply a profession or trade, or a way of life. One man who wished to become a doctor and indeed seemed to have all the qualities necessary for this profession, may have been obliged by social conditions to become a manual laborer, yet it is not all difficult for him too to live as an honest citizen and help to build God's kingdom. A young girl who never doubted she was called to be a wife and mother has been compelled by external circumstances to remain unmarried, yet she does not for this reason become one of the "lost souls" of the earth. One must however admit that a man who has set out along the wrong road only rarely experiences the creative joy and exhilaration which make life a sublime joy. Most of our contemporaries, who lead drab, joyless lives, are undoubtedly people who have — mostly through no fault of their own — followed a road which was not the right one for them. Generally speaking, it is social obligations which prevent people from finding and following the road which is right for them. Consequently, we cannot be content with merely trying to make individuals aware of this: the improvement and humanizing of the social order is, to say the least, just as urgent as the conversion of individuals. We have already asserted that a personal vocation depends closely on an individual's actual circumstances, and therefore it is incumbent upon us all to see that every man shall from the start find himself in a situation which renders it possible for him to follow his own destiny. The fact that heroic individuals fulfill their vocation in spite of all social obstacles and opposition must not serve as a pretext for us to abstain from trying to do away with these obstacles and hindrances.

* * *

However important the intermediary role played by our temporal vocation in relation to our eternal vocation, it would be mistaken to believe that the latter is a sort of logical consequence of fidelity to the former.

In order that man should be enabled to follow his transcendental calling and to attain personal union with God, he needs the new and direct intervention of God himself. God raised men above the highest peaks of human nature by giving him a share in his own life, an absolutely free gift which Christians call grace, and grace must never be confused with even the richest human qualities. Among many illustrious men well known to me the philosopher Henry

Bergson was undoubtedly one of those most richly endowed by nature as much in qualities of the heart as in those of the mind. All his work shows to what spiritual heights he was able to climb. But when Bergson found faith in Christ not only was his natural existence perfected but on that day God granted him also a share in his own divine life.

We can never assert that fidelity to our earthly duties deserves the gift of grace which enables us to discover our eternal vocation. Nothing purely natural can deserve what is supernatural, for there is a break in continuity between the two orders. Nevertheless, we remain convinced that a man's natural vocation is the most efficient means of fulfilling his transcendental vocation. It prepares human life to receive God's gift of grace. It enables us to prize God's gift at its true worth, and teaches us also how to keep faith with it. After we have heard God's call and responded to it our natural vocation will be seen as the foundation of our vocation as children of God. The Christian laborer worships and praises God while he conscientiously follows his own vocation as a laborer: the mother of a family, the shop-keeper or teacher, do the same.

* * *

Are we to understand from all this that a true vocation is something for Christians only, or at least, only for religious people, for those who are consciously in search of the transcendental? Certainly not. We have already said what ought to be thought of those who seek God without knowing who it is they are seeking. Their vocation is certainly imperfectly fulfilled but it is, at least subjectively, very real and of an unquestionable human authenticity. In innumerable cases they show such absolute devotion to their idol that one can even describe their vocation as being "subjectively" transcendental. This false transcendence assumes all the characteristics of true transcendence, so that it is very difficult at first sight to distinguish between them. Only in some extremity, as for example when in danger of death, can the idolater become aware that the ideal for which he lived is still in some way imperfect, and from this point on he will perhaps long for perfection and strive after it. But I know from personal experience that this does not always happen, and that in fact many idolaters, most distinguished for their humane qualities, remain true to their idols till the end, convinced that there is nothing more true or sublime than these.

Even those who out of cowardice or spite — Kierkegaard calls them "demoniacs" — have categorically denied God and so forfeited their transcendental vocation, are not for this reason to be considered wholly corrupt and sinful, as the Jansenists believed. Those natural gifts which God granted to them, and which are still good in themselves, will not be taken away from them. Their understanding will be open to a knowledge of the truth, their hearts will still be capable of delighting in goodness and nobility, and their minds still able to appreciate the beauty of the world. But since the natural vocation of these "demoniacs" remains undeveloped their lives will always be imperfect.

The love and magnanimity of the "demoniacs" are imprisoned in the finite and so are unable to reach their normal goal. When a man's human condition, at home or at work, leads to no transcendental condition, he must have mistaken his earthly vocation. Such a man thinks he can glorify himself, while claiming to be "just a natural man," but really in this way he belies his own nature, for a man is more than "just a natural" creature. There lies the tragedy of any humanism which as Karl Marx said, "wishes to make of men and for men the highest form of creature." The humanist may well begin as a super-optimist, but he will soon sink into the gloomiest pessimism.

In order to be truly human we must offer to God all that we have and are, that is, all that we have been given. We must place ourselves in the service of God's over-all purpose.

If we do this we shall glorify God through our own lives, and we ourselves shall become the honor and joy of creation, and we shall make our own contribution to the fulfillment of the purpose of the whole universe. Nature has indeed no other end except that of creating the necessary conditions for the birth and growth of the spirit. When the created spirit fulfills its final vocation in God, nature too will have fulfilled her own vocation. But if man, following the example of Satan, resolves to be totally independent, then he cuts himself off not only from what is higher than himself but also from his roots in the lower order of creation.

CHAPTER IV

THE ADVENTURE OF GROWTH

Human life is not a gift which we have merely to accept. Nor is it eternal. It is situated in time, and is so much concerned with becoming something else that "becoming" is as characteristic of our existence here as "being" is characteristic of eternity. Ancient and modern philosophers who declared time to be a degradation of eternity and so took "becoming" as a symbol of imperfection, were quite mistaken. In fact, man must look upon time and eternity as two different forms of duration, each of which has its own perfection. Eternity is the duration of "being," above all, the duration of God. Immutability belongs to the absolute perfection of God and, according to theologians, signifies the simultaneity of his whole being in himself. But, in order to understand this, man must not confuse divine immutability with static immobility; eternity is not just time standing still.

For creatures who fulfill their vocation in time the process of growth, of "becoming," does not denote an imperfect condition which must be remedied as soon as possible. It is on the contrary the natural condition of their existence; in fact their only true vocation is growth, and they must seek their fulfillment in this. Of all the creatures now existing those who are still in a process of transformation are more numerous than those who are in a state of immobility. The biologist knows well that a species which for any reason has ceased to develop will soon die out. The goal of all development is consequently not immobility but a still higher stage of development. A man who aspires to a state of rest and wishes to be released from this continual process of transformation is no longer truly alive; the seed of death is present in him. The evolution of nature does not lead to perfection, in the static sense as understood in Greek philosophy, but leads to man, and man questions the whole order of the universe and seek to control her latent forces and energies. With the appearance of man natural evolution has not come to an end but has been raised to a higher kind of growth, spiritual evolution.

The main difference between natural evolution and the existential development of men consists in the fact that nature proceeds as it were automatically, according to her own immanent laws or under the influence of external causes, whereas the evolution of the "nöosphere," the spiritual world, must be for the most part the work of man himself. He must rediscover himself everyday. Whoever claims to have transported himself into the sphere of eternity and to have done with the process of evolution will have implicitly renounced his true life and condemned himself to spiritual death. This means that man is not something which "is," but something which is "becoming"; in fact, man is an assignment. Whoever fails to take seriously this sense of an assignment, and to direct and control his own development, will never escape from time. Instead of mastering it he will be its slave. In any case he will always be subject to the biological, psychological, moral and sociological laws of evolution, but because his submission to these is merely passive he will not find them conducive to his own inner unity and to eternal life, but rather a cause of the disintegration and dissolution of his personality. Dilettantes and aesthetes enjoy this sort of sub-existence, although most of them imagine they are living "moments of eternity."

Unlike purely natural creatures, man not only lives, thinks and loves, but does so consciously. He is not merely a part of the evolutionary process: he plays an active role in his own evolution and as he is endowed with self-awareness and freedom he must be looked upon not merely as bearing the sign of God but as made in God's image. Consequently, he must take an active part in the shaping of his own existence and of the world around him. These human characteristics of self-awareness and freedom are evidently not elementary and universal gifts of nature. Nor are they gifts of grace, for grace follows its own laws of growth. The evolution of man presupposes a permanent struggle against nature and in search of perfection. We may conjecture that the capabilities possessed by primitive man were very imperfect. Everyone has to perfect his own powers and latent capacities.

Moreover, man can in no moment of his life be sure that he has done all that he is capable of doing. As long as we live in time we must everyday and in every moment continue the struggle for perfection and for the increase of self-awareness and freedom: this is the main purpose of human evolution. Although man fulfills his vocation through a creative process he does not create himself. He could not have created his own awareness and freedom out of nothing, for human creation is different from divine creation. What he is to become is already present in himself; he is already, in a certain sense, that person, because from his birth onwards he has always had the possibility of becoming it. There does not exist anywhere in the world mere abstract growth without something which grows. A personality is built up and molded only because it is naturally capable of growth. In spite of his constant and never completely perfected evolution a man always remains the same man. If this were not so, there would be no such thing as personality. The Mr. Smith I met today and the Mr. Smith who last year rendered me a valuable service, would then have nothing in common with each other, and I should have no reason to be grateful to him — in fact, I should no longer be the same man to whom the service was rendered. If we accept the hypothesis of blind evolution, as many philosophers have done, it is impossible to speak of vocation, responsibility and commitment. But our innermost experience confirms, despite all sophistry, the permanent identity of our own personality as well as the permanent identity of others. We are absolutely certain that we have remained morally and ontologically the same people in spite of our evolutionary existence. We obey the imperative call, heard in our innermost hearts, to communicate with others and with the world, and to develop our own personalities. On the other hand, we are also aware that there is in every person something unique, eternal and sacred which we must cherish and protect. Our own identity and the identity of others are to be treated with respect: God himself respects our personal identity. It is indeed indisputable that even in the most sudden and radical conversions personal identity is preserved. One does not need to have made a special study of vocations to recognize in Paul, the intrepid apostle, Saul, the fanatical persecutor of Christians. Augustine, Francis of Assisi, Ignatius Loyola, Charles de Foucauld, Paul Claudel, Charles Péguy and innumerable other famous or unknown converts were faithful to their own identity, in spite of the tremendous transformation worked in them by God. Would Augustine have spoken of God's grace so persuasively and in such glowing terms if he had severed himself completely from the Augustine who had such a comprehensive experience of human powerlessness and incapacity to attain truth and moral virtue by his own strength alone? People of our own time, who have a proper respect for all that is earthly and temporal, find themselves much in sympathy with the hermit of the Sahara, Charles de Foucauld, for this reason especially, that he remained always the same man who before his conversion had loved the world so passionately and had undertaken dangerous and important explorations. The young troubadour of Assisi did not renounce his romantic love of nature and of poetry when he became the holy Francis. In all these men we see a mighty development, but it was they themselves who had developed. Psychologically speaking, it is not quite true to say that the "old man" had died in Paul or in Augustine: he still lived on in the "new man," but he had risen to a higher plane.

The banality of our daily life transforms us so totally that nothing, or at least very little, remains of our former selves. I have several times felt bitterly disappointed when, after a long separation, I have met a friend of former years and have been obliged to ascertain that he was so greatly altered that I could hardly recognize him as the same personality. It was impossible to re-establish our former mutual understanding: he had become another man. But in such a case a person loses only his moral identity, not his ontological identity. In fact, provided he has the courage to listen to it, a man's own inner experience convinces him, even when he has become lost in the humdrum daily round, that in spite of all vicissitudes he has remained the same person.

* * *

The combination of permanent evolution with personal identity in a man's soul seems one of the greatest paradoxes of our existence: the more real our life is the more swiftly and thoroughly it becomes transformed and the more permanent is the identity of the self. Philosophers were for too long occupied with studying the nature of man and enumerating his supposed characteristics. From this point of view naturally more emphasis was laid on the study of his being, and less on the study of his activity. This does not mean that we attach little importance to the study of being, or think it may be dispensed with: it certainly formed the core of all ancient philosophy, to which we have much cause to feel grateful because it taught us how to think scientifically.

On the other hand, it was meditation, religious meditation, which drew innumerable saints nearer to God. Our vocation as men of this age precludes pure speculation about the eternal and immutable: it requires us to act in order to transform the world and mankind. We know also that our life here is to be perfected not in eternity but in time, and that it must comply with the laws of evolution.

Moreover, however justifiable and pleasant it is to contemplate the beauty of the world and the wonder of our own personalities, it is more important for us to discover the conditions and laws of our evolution and — since it is so closely tied up with universal evolution — to discover this also. Only by so doing shall we be able to fulfill our own destiny and contribute to the fulfillment of that of others. It is indeed the principal task of pedagogy to advance human progress. Certainly teachers have an imperative duty to discover the fundamental character of the child entrusted to them. Upon this foundation, which is the object of all character study and psychoanalysis, must the man, which the child is to become, be built. All that will be the future adult is already present in the child, as the oak tree is present in the acorn. But in order that the acorn may become a mighty tree it must grow in a favorable climate and in good conditions. In order that the child may become a man and fulfill his vocation, his teachers must study the conditions and laws of his development. It is therefore of the greatest importance for all teachers to ascertain the child's potentialities and capacities, and above all to train him gradually to undertake the direction of his own development. This is the proper task of pedagogy and of psychosynthesis. Not only vocation experts and psychologists but all men who have to guide and lead others, or even themselves alone, find it useful and necessary to have some knowledge of the laws of growth.

As man does not live alone in a hot house but in the company of other men, naturally it is not enough for him to know the subjective conditions of his own development. The best intentioned efforts and the most brilliant pedagogic methods can do nothing as long as men live in a society where injustice reigns, where mothers of families and children must work in factories, where large sections suffer from material insecurity and excessive class distinctions. The salvation, the social salvation, of the individual can hardly be achieved except through the common welfare of society and so of all men. Consequently, individual progress must go forward step by step with social progress. A true life must be sought on the individual and social planes simultaneously. On the other hand, man must also understand that social progress is only practicable if it promotes the progress of individual men, in fact, if it expressly sets out to do just that. If social advancement is an end in itself, as is the case with materialistic communism, then it can only bring unhappiness to men and so lose all its justification.

On the personal plane growth aims at the even more profound spiritualization of life, the conquest of an even more perfect freedom. We must become aware of our duties and responsibilities, and of ourselves. It may well be, as pessimists believe, that from the moral point of view the men of today are no better than their forefathers of the year 1000, but undoubtedly in all they do, for good or ill, they now act more deliberately, and so their responsibility is increased. This unquestionably denotes some progress in the intellectual sphere.

On the social plane man has until now allowed progress to become too dependent on the laws of economics, and for this reason he has been unable to direct his own evolution harmoniously.

Explorations and discoveries, reforms and revolutions, are

generally only justifiable in so far as they promote social justice and peaceful relations between individuals and between peoples. Social evolution must strive to shape an order in which personal freedom may flourish. It must not draw such narrow boundaries as to render personal progress difficult or even impossible. The perfect society of the termites must not be adopted as an example for human society.

Human existence — whether considered from the individual, social, biological, psychological, moral or intellectual point of view, consists, as we have said, in perpetual expansion and growth. Its present hour has no pause for rest, no sense of finality: the present is but a stream flowing towards the future. Heraclitus was so struck by the unceasing movement of all created things that he could assert that a man never bathed twice in the same river. Since then, with the knowledge we now have of the evolution of man himself, we dare go a step further and say: "The same man never bathes twice." Nevertheless, as we have already asserted, there is no break of continuity between the bather of yesterday and the bather of today. Man's life is not merely a series of dissolving situations; man is also spirit and as such he enjoys a permanence in his being which mere things have not.

The awareness of our evolutionary condition will give us no cause for an inferiority complex, or for self-denigration. In opposition to those philosophers who consider immutability to be the mark of perfection, we are firmly convinced that man's continual state of growth and transformation represents no weakness or imperfection. When we study the matter more closely and carefully we shall see the nobility and beauty of perpetual growth. Our Creator is not to be reproached for not having made men perfect from the start. The fact that he has entrusted our perfection to us must on the contrary be seen as a proof of divine generosity. Kierkegaard agreed with Lessing: If God had held in his right hand the attainment of perfect truth and in his left hand the laborious search for truth, he would have opened his left hand to those he loved.

What is valid for the search for truth is equally valid for physical, moral and spiritual growth. As long as we live in time, to secure total possession means for us not fulfillment but spiritual death. The rejection of the laws of time leads us, not to eternity but to corruption.

It is especially worthy of note that God's own Son, when he became Man, did not come to us in perfect manhood, in possession of all the riches of human nature — for many years, we are told, he "increased in wisdom and in stature." He thought it was right for him, while he lived in time, to live according to the laws of time. And the whole story of God's relations with men bears the same mark of growth and development.

Mankind cannot achieve perfection in one bound, any more than the individual man can do so. If we read the Old and the New Testament without taking into consideration the constant spiritual development of mankind, we shall hardly be able to understand any part of it, for it will all seem full of contradictions and absurdities. The divine truth about man is only gradually revealed, as man progresses spiritually and socially. The coming of Christ did not put an end to spiritual growth. On the contrary, it gave it a new impetus. Certainly all God's gifts to man are already even now at his disposal but he is not yet "big" enough to know how to use or enjoy them. In the course of time the revealed truth will be ever more widely and profoundly understood and the moral lessons of the Gospel more faithfully observed in general practice.

There is hardly anything more contrary to true living than perfectionism, whether this appears on the intellectual, moral or spiritual plane, because perfection is frequently used to cover up spiritual suicide. Paul himself implored the Corinthians not to think of themselves as having already attained Christian perfection, but as still striving for it. As we have already mentioned, Kierkegaard, who had a particularly strong sense of the mystery of spiritual growth, denied that anyone had the right to call himself a Christian: there has only ever been one real Christian, Christ himself, and our Christianity is merely a more or less intense effort to become Christian. It is indeed most interesting to try to discover what the Christian religion really is, and for this reason dogma has its own justification, but it is nevertheless inadequate because our real problem is to discover how we as individuals, just as we are and with all that goes to make us as we are, may become Christians.

* * *

If human growth and development were uninterrupted and harmonious it would be comparatively easy to renounce rest and all that we have already attained in order to cooperate fully in the process of development, and to be proudly aware of our human condition of permanent growth. In practice, however, our development is a dialectical process: it is accomplished through struggles and contradictions.

Our own experience and the history of the world tell us that men, whether considered as individuals or *en masse,* achieve progress only through crises and revolutions. The condition of man is one of continual "growing pains." The discovery of every new situation, and the revelation of every new existential value, always entail a painful process of dying. Let us, for example, consider conversion to the Christian faith: the spiritual development is here particularly rapid. The convert discovers and acquires new values, with hitherto unsuspected possibilities for the development of his intelligence, his feelings and his heart. When the conversion is sudden, as it was with Paul, we feel as if we had in a few moments taken an enormous stride forwards and upwards. Naturally, when conversion brings with it such a sudden development no spiritually mature man would resist it. But becoming a Christian also implies the death of the "old man," the renunciation of many former habits, and of some much prized pleasures. The *Confessions* of St. Augustine are a glowing account of the dramatic struggle in his soul between the new man who had been born and the old man who refused to die.

Spiritual growth postulates the rejection of all prejudices, all craving for power and all intolerance, but we learn from experience that it is not all easy constantly to preserve a spirit of open-mindedness and receptivity.

Although some passages from one phase to another are achieved peacefully in general we must resign ourselves to a complete break with the past. The most disconcerting thing, however, is that this break which is often so painful generally leads to nothing final but only to the necessity of making other sacrifices which may be even more painful. And the upward climb is seldom uninterrupted. In all regions of human progress we already know from experience that we are frequently obliged to descend from the heights we have won. We are full of enthusiasm to climb to the summit, but we stumble over obstacles and have to turn back. Indeed, sometimes the descent is much more rapid than the upward climb, and we find ourselves at a lower point than the one we started from. So our progress turns out to be a permanent state of beginning all over again! But if we do not wish to commit spiritual suicide we must realize that there is no other way and that we dare not let ourselves be discouraged but must set out once more on the steep upward road. The important thing is to try every time to reach a higher point than the one we reached before.

The faint-hearted are far too much afraid of the dangers inseparable from this process of growth. They fear its continual stress and strain. Repose seems to them a much safer state, and they find it very alluring. Cessation of effort seems to them the hallmark of success. They do their best to sit or lie in the safest place, and they try to cling to an unmoving present. The illusion of having thus "opted out" of time may comfort them for a while, but soon they will realize that they have chosen not an eternal present but the way to their own dissolution. They have abdicated control over their own development and now they must vegetate like inanimate things. This leads to the decadence of individuals, classes and nations.

CHAPTER V

FREEDOM AND THE PROCESS OF LIBERATION

The fulfillment of one's own vocation, a life full of adventurous enterprise — is all this anything more than fine words? In order that it may be more, and different, man must at least to some extent be master of his own life and activity. He must be capable of choosing his own goal and discerning the right way to it. Undoubtedly none of the natural creatures of our universe has a similar power over its own development. However highly developed they may be they cannot free themselves from the automatism of natural laws: they have no power to create or to invent. They can modify themselves and develop, and indeed sometimes they may reach a high degree of evolution and perfection, but they themselves play no active part in this evolution and transformation. All is accomplished either according to the immanent laws of their own nature or through the intervention of external causes.

These alone are capable sometimes of breaking through

the vicious circle of determinism in which all natural creatures are imprisoned.

Is this true also of man's evolution? During the last century numerous scientific schools believed this was so, and some of these even today still have their followers among psychologists and sociologists. According to them, man's freedom is a mere illusion: he is born willy-nilly and he will die without giving his consent to death. All that happens during the months or years which intervene between these two landmarks, birth and death, has only the appearance of freedom. As we do not yet know all the causes which affect our lives, we may think we are in control of them when this is not really so. The climate of our native land, the economic conditions of our families, the supply and demand situation and technical prowess all have, the determinists aver, as strong an influence over the individual and social evolution of men as peculiarities of soil, water and light have over the growth of plants. If a working man's son, born in poverty, who must from his cradle onwards bear on his weak shoulders the hardships of his proletarian condition, becomes in spite of all this a famous scientist or an eminent statesman, it is only because these determining causes have been disturbed by chance. But even then he is not free because he has become subject to another chain of causes which work just as mechanically upon his destiny as did the original causes which chance had disturbed. Thus the determinists see only one possibility of ameliorating the destiny of individual men and of mankind as a whole: we must try to alter these external circumstances which determine them. Those philosophers who are not interested in ontological freedom but particularly, if not exclusively, concerned with economic determinism, are sincerely convinced that if they alter the whole system of supply and demand they will alter man also, and thus radically transform the destiny of all mankind. For them the process is just the same as in the vegetable world: when a tree or a flower begins to wither we change its soil.

In our opinion the deterministic conception of man has for the last hundred years done much to bring about the decadence of the West. It is also the main obstacle to progress in Indian and other Asiatic countries. It encourages indolence and saps the will. Even Christians, at least in the practical sphere of daily life, have not always succeeded in protecting themselves from sociological and psychological determinism, and on this foundation they have built up an entirely false conception of divine providence.

The Marxists are quite convinced that human progress is irrevocably determined by the mechanization of productive power. They call upon the proletariat to abolish all existing systems of production and to replace them with new methods, and they have no doubt whatever that this revolution will bring about the happiness of mankind. But our already sufficiently long experience of the Marxist system in Russia makes us very sceptical about this: the economic system there is very different from that of the old capitalist world, but there is no sign of man's happiness having been thereby more successfully achieved.

In opposition to the vicious circle of determinism, with its impossibilities and inconsistencies, existentialists like Heidegger and Sartre, and their pupils and imitators, loudly proclaim man's absolute freedom. Freedom, they say, is not merely his most characteristic attribute but an integral part of his being. Man is freedom, rather in the same sense that God, according to St. John, is love. Sartre asserts that freedom is not something added to our nature but is made of the very same stuff. Several existential conceptions of freedom are acceptable to us too, but we must reject systematic exaggerations because they are totally opposed to the reality of our experience. According to existential theory man is absolutely free, the only unrestricted master of his own life and of his position in the world. He is free to invest himself and the universe with any meaning he wishes: he is free to be everything but bound. Sartre's freedom is neither the gift of a transcendent God nor something won by man himself: it is his doom. "I am condemned to freedom," he said. This absolute freedom, however, is not creative because it is due fundamentally to man's nothingness. He is free because he has no real being: he merely exists.

If we follow this thesis of Sartre's to its logical conclusion we see that our freedom is merely apparent and leads us back to radical determinism. For what can this freedom be which we cannot renounce, to which we are doomed? If we are conditioned to freedom then all our actions are only apparently free.

*   *   *

Philosophers have indulged in endless speculation about freedom considered as free will *(liberum arbitrium)*. According to this *a priori* supposition freedom must be either totally accepted or denied: the arguments for one position are apparently as conclusive as those for the other.

We do not wish to seek the proofs of his freedom in the "nature" of man, for man is free only in so far as he is not "natural." We look for them in his activities. What can we then learn from interior and exterior experience about freedom and determinism with regard to man's activities? We may accept Aristotle's old distinction between a man's activity *(actus hominis)* and human activity *(actus humani)*. The functioning of our stomach, heart and other bodily organs has little to do with our will but follows the same physiological laws which govern those same activities in the most highly developed mammals. Our intentions, wishes and projects have only a slight influence over our bodily organs: these latter are "human activities" in which we enjoy very little freedom. But they are not totally separated from psychic activity because various spiritual states can make our heart beat faster or affect our digestion. But when we are working with our hands or brain, delivering a speech or making certain gestures, we are acting according to a preconceived plan or intention. Whether this plan and this intention be more or less conscious and explicit nevertheless they always make these actions those of a man (*actus homini*). Before we embark upon any enterprise we conceive it as possible, desirable or useful, and at the same moment our minds are aware of our freedom to act or not to act. A captive is not in a position to act deliberately, but can only act mechanically or instinctively. His words can be hardly more expressive than the chatterings of a parrot and his work hardly more creative than the mechanical movements of a machine.

In a man's soul the source of all creative power is freedom, and every creative act offers us a new proof or our own freedom and of that of others. The intimate connection between freedom and creation prevents us from considering the highly developed instinct of many animals as a first glimmering of free will. However highly developed an instinct can be it can create nothing and can find no really new solution. Animal psychology has made great progress in recent years and we now know that some animals are instinctively capable of amazing actions which sometimes seem to surpass the achievements of free creation. Yet instinct produces only a more or less automatic repetition or movement which can be explained by reference to Pavlov's law of reflex action. Between the most highly developed instinct and minimal freedom there exists the same difference as that between the *nöosphere* and the biosphere. Instinct always works for the good of the individual or the race. On the contrary freedom gives man the fearsome power to work for his own unhappiness and for that of his race. The discovery of the atom bomb is particularly instructive in this connection. It is obvious that here we see a particularly forcible proof of man's creative power — but this same power is also the cause of the greatest threat to the survival of the whole human race. With the discovery of the atom bomb we have attained a higher degree of freedom than ever before. If we continue on the way we have chosen we do so deliberately, and we now have the power to destroy ourselves. Sad to say, there exists also the danger that this freedom to achieve self-destruction belongs also to a single individual who may refuse to take into account the fact that all the others wish to survive. Our spiritual evolution is not yet sufficiently advanced for the moral conscience of the individual to be fully in harmony with the moral conscience of mankind as a whole.

Human freedom is not perfect; nor is it a conquest made once and for all time. Followers and opponents of freedom have often followed the wrong road because they think of it as something absolute. Certainly, since man came into this world, everyone is born with all he needs to become a real man: it is already latent in him. Since freedom is one of the primary attributes of the soul it is understandable that freedom also must be present in germ in a man's nature. But this is merely the metaphysics of the question. Men are not condemned to freedom; they are called to it, in order to develop it themselves. The gradual development of his freedom means for man a victory over nature. To become a man and to become free are two aspects of the same spiritual growth. We are not all equally men; nor are we all equally free. Some eminent representatives of our race attain such a sublime degree of freedom that apparently they can control not only their spiritual life but even to some extent their physical life too. Yet, even St. Francis of Assisi and Mahatma Gandhi did not enjoy absolute freedom. This statement can only surprise people who are accustomed to think of men and freedom in the abstract and within a concept of eternity.

Among the greatest philosophers it was Hegel who most clearly and explicitly stressed the relativity of human freedom, without however denying its existence. In his *Phenomenology of Mind* (Torch Books tb 1303, 1967, Harper and Row) he examines the freedom of the landowner who has slaves to serve him. Because the master himself is not obliged to do any menial work, he believes he is perfectly free. But his own freedom is only possible because other men are slaves, and therefore deprived of their freedom. The master's freedom itself is only apparent because he is totally dependent upon his slaves and so is in reality subject to them. Consequently, the independence of men is always an illusion and Hegel prefers to speak, not about freedom itself but about various kinds of freedom: we enjoy certain kinds of freedom but no true freedom. Although Hegel's analysis is not entirely meaningless we must note that he is considering man only in the abstract. In order to understand man's true nature we must leave the plane of abstract speculation and move to the existential plane, where man is considered only in the circumstances in which he actually lives. The real freedom of men depends on the conditions of their environment, which may help or hinder its development.

We have already insisted that we are conditioned by the world of nature which surrounds us and by all its powers of light and darkness and the whole vast might of the universe in the midst of which we have to live. Nature does not submit to us without a struggle and we cannot with impunity treat it just as we please.

But when we are aware of our freedom and have already raised it to a relatively high degree then we owe this freedom of ours to the very struggles in which we are engaged in order to dominate nature. If the natural world had spontaneously placed itself at our disposal and offered no resistance, we might quite possibly have never become aware of our freedom. From the ontological point of view all creatures are either free or bound, but from the moral and psychological point of view human beings enjoy only a relative freedom, which we find in the very effort we make to attain it.

Man is not alone in the lap of nature. He is conditioned by his relations with other men, that is, with other freedoms. From the very start of his conscious life he comes up against other wills which either oppose him or assist him. As happens also with children, he begins to win his freedom when he learns to say "no." When he comes up against another person's freedom this other freedom may share its strength with him and persuade him to over step his natural limitations, and it may urge him forward to show him the way which leads through liberating struggles to true freedom. But it does not always turn out like this. Other men's freedoms may look upon mine as an interloper or a rival and may consider it their duty in self-defense to oppose my efforts to establish my own freedom. Or perhaps they will never admit that I have a personal vocation of my own, and so they may try to force me to follow their way and so frustrate my own puny efforts to find freedom. In any case it is impossible for us to ignore the freedoms of others — we have to reckon with them.

Perhaps the sociological and political conditions of the civilization in which we live are more important even than the struggle between individual freedoms. For many the burden of these sociological conditions — whether inherited or acquired — is so oppressive that their freedom can be attained only within an extremely constricted circle. For the syphilitic youth who is the descendant of several generations of alcoholics and was born and bred in a poor ragpicker's hovel, what can the word freedom mean? His chances of leading a real existence are from the start very slight, if not altogether nonexistent. In the majority of such cases we need be neither an astrologer nor a fortune-teller to be able to predict this man's future. Individual freedom remains undoubtedly the privilege of the minority, at least until the conditions for collective freedom have been created. If all are not equally ready to contribute to the creation of these conditions it is first of all because they think that the freedom of the minority, to which they themselves belong, requires the suppression of the freedom of the majority. So freedom for traditional liberalism means every individual having the right to use his own property according to his own judgment, and without any responsibility towards all other members of the community. In extreme cases this conception of freedom includes also the right to commit suicide, or to submit to an abortion, or the right to burn wheat in order to maintain its high price, without any thought for the millions of people who lack the bare necessities of life. On the spiritual plane liberals logically claim the right to say or to write everything they wish, without caring what the consequences may be for others.

Is it to be wondered at that the result of such a misuse of freedom has been the present "freedom crisis" which has led to totalitarianism of the Left or of the Right? Historically speaking, the official destruction of social solidarity dates from the French Revolution of 1789, for it was through this revolution that the middle classes won their own political freedom. The Declaration of Human Rights, and the many constitutions of states which it inspired, prohibited — even in the name of the freedom of the individual — the right to form free associations.

Only the rich and powerful could benefit from such an abstract freedom, while the poor and humble were still subject to the implacable laws of production and profit. In a world in which money was the most highly prized commodity the poor had hardly any share in economic progress. Although the nations were rich the majority of their people lived in poverty and distress. Moreover, the much vaunted intellectual freedom could mean little to uneducated people who were hardly capable of forming their own opinions, which they imbibed from whatever newspaper they read or from the milieu in which they lived. Even political freedom, with universal suffrage and parliamentary democracy, seemed to the humble masses a trick by which they were handed over to the demagogues and the power of propaganda. This state of things must be borne in mind if we wish rightly to understand the success of Communist or Fascist agitators among these people. They really believed they had nothing to lose by exchanging their much extolled freedom for the promise of security and prosperity.

If we are really convinced that freedom is a great boon to

man, then we must not be content to wrest only our personal freedom from the clutches of all pervading determinism, for the conquest of social freedom is for us all a binding duty. How can we be content with a world in which extreme material poverty, insecurity, and the impossibility of leading lives worthy of men, rob innumerable individuals of the chance to live in freedom? There are so many people in the modern industrialized world, in which the economist is concerned about over-production, and in the most highly developed countries (even the "socialist" states) who enjoy hardly any more material or spiritual liberty than did the slaves and serfs of the past. In many respects the slaves' living conditions were actually better than those of the modern proletariat, for although slaves and serfs had no legal independence they belonged to a community which did not usually leave them in the lurch when they were in need.

If they were Christians they had at least the certainty that no earthly slavery could deprive them of their spiritual freedom. Today, on the other hand, the "common man" is endowed with every possible juridical freedom but feels he is alone in the world, understanding hardly anything about his destiny or about the dangers to which he feels helplessly exposed. He has the sensation of wandering around in the world like a disconnected atom. The ultimate freedom he thinks he still possesses is freedom to revolt against all order.

Marxist communism promises to free mankind finally from all spiritual and material "alienation." But in reality it robs men even of the scanty freedom which capitalist materialism has left them. In fact, in the name of efficiency, communism demands from its adherents the renunciation of all private judgment and all creative initiative. In the countries where it has seized power the pressure which it brings to bear on individuals and peoples is worse than the oppressive rule of all the capitalist and colonial powers. Imprisonment, forced labor and systematically organized propaganda are used as means of expropriating all personal freedom. The worst result is that the masses in these countries no longer know that such freedom exists, for communism has to some extent succeeded in suffocating even the will to be free. If at this price it were really possible to free mankind from all material exploitation and poverty, would this imply any real progress in the spiritual sphere? The Soviet writer Dudinzev, in his novel *Man Does Not Live by Bread Alone* (Dutton, 1957)— which, thanks to the relative liberalization of the post-Stalin period, he was allowed to publish—answers this question with a categorical "No."

I know very well what the faithful communist will say in reply: "The total suppression of personal freedom is, during the preliminary stage of a communist regime, a temporary measure which is necessary in order to clear all obstacles from the path of collective freedom. The proletarian himself must be re-educated before he is able to enjoy personal freedom within collective freedom. In order that the collective freedom won by revolution may not be lost before this re-education can be completed, a dictatorship, or even a rule of terror, is an indispensable necessity.

Before men can be allowed to think and act in total freedom they must be inculcated with the principles of thought and action taught by the party or by the communist state.

This conception implicitly inspires the theory of the radical distinction to be drawn between the means and the end. It presupposes that the all-powerful totalitarian state may abolish the state and that suppression may abolish suppression. But this presupposition is contradicted by all psychological and sociological experience. The means and their end are bound in a close reciprocal interdependence: it is absolutely impossible to attain truth through falsehood and freedom through slavery.

Because freedom is the principal attribute of a spiritual being who has a vocation to fulfill, a man has even less right to renounce it than to renounce any other innate or acquired attribute. If he does he will decline not only morally but ontologically, and sink to the level of an inanimate thing.

A man is free only in so far as he is truly human, that is, in so far as he raises himself above the natural state. But not all men are able to raise themselves to the same height, and so it is understandable that all do not enjoy the same degree of freedom. The mass of men who live their humdrum daily lives as slaves to pseudo-traditions, routines, prejudices and intellectual formulae, conforming in feeling and action to the rules and criteria of their milieus, enjoy only a very relative freedom. They have hardly any personal plan for living or any personal preferences, and being without any sense of a more sublime purpose they follow their daily routine without demur. It is the existence of these men which naturally gives the determinists good arguments for casting doubt upon human freedom, or even for denying it altogether.

The more genuine an existence the greater its freedom. Men like Francis of Assisi and Mahatma Gandhi succeeded in attaining almost perfect freedom. With them not only all human activities but even the activities of individuals were considered in the light of a higher purpose. Their immediate needs as individuals or as members of a race were almost always under their control, so that in even their purely bodily functions they enjoyed a certain freedom. Whoever wishes to find out from experience whether man is free or not — or better, whether he is capable of freeing himself — and what human freedom really means, must learn not from primitive people or the general mass of men, but from men like these who have reached the peak of freedom, the highest stage in the spiritual world.

However slight a part freedom may play in many drab and dull lives, it is nevertheless indisputable that no one is entirely without it. Even the insane enjoy a certain freedom, at least from time to time. If a man is deprived of liberty in every department of his life he ceases to be a man.

We must not confuse freedom with our so-called "free will" *(liberum arbitrium)*, as both supporters and opponents of deterministic theories so eagerly and frequently do. Free will consists of man's imputed capacity to choose between two things or courses of action which are both equally within his power to do. In the strict sense of the word there is hardly such a thing as free will, for in fact we are all constantly influenced by motives and inducements which incline us towards this or that thing or action. Moreover there are often also external circumstances which leave free will very little scope. A man condemned to death is not free to choose between life and death. Nevertheless, he does not cease to be free for he can accept pain and death with an untroubled spirit, as Socrates did, or submit to them passively, or even struggle against them.

For psychologists and moralists this distinction between theoretical free will and real freedom is extremely important. It enables us first of all to understand, at least to some extent, how it is that God is supremely free, although he does not have to make any deliberate choice between good and evil. Many Christians, accustomed to confuse freedom with free will, find it hard to understand that Christ and the Virgin Mary were truly free although, because of their special vocation, no choice between good and evil or even between the good and the less good, was open to them. In spite of this they were both perfectly free, incomparably freer than we could ever be. Most of the obstacles which constrict our freedom and impede its full development were absent in Christ and in Mary. Therefore the part played by determinist factors in their lives was exceptionally slight and most probably reduced to specific physiological causes. It will be the same with us all when we leave this realm of time and enter eternity. Then we shall so clearly recognize what is good that we shall never again desire what is evil. But our freedom will thereby be neither abolished nor diminished: it will instead reach its fullness. Our wills will no longer be subject to interior or exterior influences, and our love for God will be supreme and absolutely free.

Even our passions, now so constricted, will then have perfect freedom. We shall love God and all that is good passionately, and nothing will ever be able to detract from this love. Free will is therefore not the whole of freedom but only a part of it, although in our temporal state it seems more important.

Another mistake which is particularly common in our century is that of identifying freedom with the arbitrary use of power. We have already referred to this error on the social plane: it is the characteristic claim of liberalism that everyone has the right to dispose of himself and of his property freely without having to render an account to anyone else. A certain philosophy, widely disseminated in many novels in the period between the two great wars, recognized only the arbitrary use of power as true freedom. Lafcadio, a character in one of André Gide's novels, believed he was perpetrating a fine free action when he murdered an unknown man in the train, simply because he had no reason for killing him. If he had killed him in order to seize his victim's money or because he bore him some grudge, his action would, according to Gide, have lost its quality of freedom and so would have been unworthy of a superman. In reality, arbitrariness is not an essential characteristic of free action. A man's motives, however numerous and impelling they may be, do not destroy his freedom of action. He himself may assign to this or that factor the character of a motive.

On the other hand, motives are never the decisive causes of human action. We see the proof of this in the fact that these same factors have often been present without moving us to action. Before the fatal night of his conversion the poet Paul Claudel had often attended Christmas Mass without experiencing anything out of the ordinary. Yet on that particular night the Christmas Mass was the motive of his conversion — only because his freedom, illumined by grace, had brought him to this conclusion, although the decision had been formed in his subconsciousness.

* * *

Freedom is such an essential human possession that the spiritually mature man will never part with it at any price. How many children in the Soviet Union and elsewhere still prefer the misery and insecurity of the high road to the relative comfort and security of the reformatory or orphanage! Those reformatories for young criminals, into which has not been possible to introduce a free relationship between teacher and pupil, may even offer their inmates all the advantages of good middle-class life but they cannot prevent the boys from wishing to seize every favorable opportunity to run away. Many poor old people prefer to beg or to live half-starved and sleep under bridges rather than give up their freedom in order to enter a home for the aged. We must not be irritated by this apparently absurd behavior: it is only because the longing for freedom has not yet been lost that we dare, in spite of all, remain optimistic about the future of mankind.

Because of its need to have the possibility of initiative, freedom cannot long be content with narrow or restricted boundaries. Sooner or later it will seize the opportunity to break out. Then we have the danger of anarchy or of excessive license. It is general experience that educational methods which lay too much emphasis on coercion and not enough on freedom produce hooligans and debauchery, just as dictatorships and tyrannies are generally the precursors of disorder and anarchy. Bloody revolutions are not so much the work of agitators as of men of order who place too much trust in police and armies.

Since man is a free agent it is impossible to foretell his destiny according to the so-called laws of science. Psychological laws never have the same precision and certainty as biological or physio-chemical laws. Depth psychologists and students of character may well assert that a certain man, because of his particular past or temperament, will most probably in a given situation behave in a predictable manner. This may be true of all the cases examined by scientists, and may even be a general rule, but there is no guarantee that the man in question, whose objective circumstances are well known to us, will act or react to these circumstances in the way we expect. His freedom always offers him the possibility of discovering an original way of acting or behaving that no scientific study can foresee.

The same thing happens with sociological determinism which the Marxists in particular use and misuse in their systems. Naturally we do not intend to doubt or to belittle the influence which, for example, the situation of supply and demand exerts over the philosophical conception of the world, the so-called "ideological superstructure." It is indisputable that politics, literature, art, morals and even the religious customs of any given people and in any given age bear some relation to the economic conditions in which the people live. In actual fact many analyses of historical materialism correspond to reality, but if a particularly powerful freedom appears then all our expectations grounded on determinism are deceived. According to the analyses of Karl Marx, for example, in order that a people may be ripe for proletarian revolution it must necessarily first experience the capitalist organization of the economy and possess a well organized and industrialized proletariat. The intervention of a man like Lenin nevertheless sufficed to create the first Communist state in the world out of a backward and still half feudal Russia where the industrial workers formed hardly a percentage of the population. On the contrary the situations in Italy in 1922 and in Germany in 1933 were objectively quite favorable to a communist seizure of power, but the freedom of men like Mussolini and Hitler had not been sufficiently taken into account.

Naturally we do not deny — although we regret it — that the social evolution of western countries during the last two hundred years has been dominated by the laws of sociological determinism. There is, however, no compelling necessity for this. Today men have become the victims of economic forces just because they have lost their belief in freedom, and even lost some of their desire for it. In order to be able to resist the threat of totalitarianism, from the Left or the Right, it is absolutely necessary to teach men to prize freedom as their most precious spiritual possession. They must learn to love it in every department of their own lives and to try to create new forms of communal life which may encourage individual as well as collective freedom.

It is extremely important and imperative for modern man to recover his faith in freedom. The damage caused by its abuse is certainly obvious to us all. Men seem today, moreover, too tired and too de-vitalized to resist the temptation to barter their freedom for a political and social order which will offer them security against all the perils of existence. The rest we long for is not thought of as the fruit of personal effort and conquest but as a bonus bestowed upon us by some power outside ourselves. The successes and continual recurrences of all kinds of totalitarianism can be explained by the preference tired and disillusioned men feel for abstract and impersonal order rather than for free creation. Unfortunately many people are not yet sufficiently convinced that any pleasure not won by our free efforts but more or less passively accepted soon becomes a torment. The masses find it normal and desirable that leaders and other prominent personalities should issue all the commands, which they have merely to obey.

We do not wish to put all the blame on leaders and prominent personalities, for they can assert their will to power only in so far as the masses of cowardly and disillusioned people allow them to do so. Some of them may even have the best intentions and assume the responsibility of power less for motives of ambition than out of compassion for the dispirited masses. But the temptation to substitute their own arbitrary will for the dwindling freedom of the people sometimes proves so strong that even the best dictators soon become tyrants. Almost inevitably this way leads to a cruel despotism and eventually to a collective catastrophe. The chief crime of Communist materialism is precisely its claim to compel men to accept a happiness imposed from without. Even if the Communist experiment were entirely successful men would draw no benefit from it because they would be deprived of their freedom, and this compulsory happiness would because of its uniformity be quite inhuman, like the happiness of bees in a hive. Certainly we have no right, out of cowardice or sloth, to opt out of the struggle for an ever more perfect freedom.

The fearful see more or less clearly that true freedom would prevent them from lingering in slothful ease and security, and would mean committing themselves to unending toil, for their lives would be an unending series of new enterprises. The lives of many saints, heroes and other "real" men are, however, the proof that even the most painful afflictions, if freely accepted, lose their power to depress us and may even inspire the most sublime joy and most profound existential satisfaction.

We have already several times insisted that freedom must never deteriorate into despotism or anarchy. Young people, new classes and new nations are sorely tempted to use their freedom for the arbitrary assertion of their own autonomy and power. They assert their own claim to unbridled freedom and refuse to reckon with the freedom of others or with the cosmic laws which condition and govern their freedom. Sartre, the mouthpiece for the youth of his day, asserts that man can only be free if he has neither a motherland nor a family, nor indeed any religion or moral code. But if we follow this trend of thought we fail to understand that human freedom must necessarily be conditioned and committed. History shows that a nation which, in order to assert its own freedom, robs other nations of theirs often ends in ruin or slavery. Freedom certainly creates dynamic power in men, but in order that this power may be creative and not destructive it must be used intelligently. The intelligence teaches freedom how to proceed forward and upward and supplies its working rule.

The consciousness of the limitations of human freedom in no way impedes its creative force. On the contrary, only under these conditions is freedom able to concentrate all her strength on the task which is within her power. Hegel had already discovered that man is at one and the same time both free and conditioned, and that it is only by struggling against these limitations that he becomes free. At the center of every real life the war between freedom and determinism creates the dialectic of human progress. Descartes also was well aware of this diarchy, freedom-determinism, but he believed that man is free in his will and conditioned in his emotional life. In order to be able to establish with any certainty which human actions are free and which are pre-determined we must distinguish between these two sources, the will and the passions. Then it will be quite easy to judge the worth of our actions and to establish our degree of responsibility. We know what sort of use, and misuse, the casuists of the seventeenth century made of this theory.

A closer study of human motives enables us, however, to ascertain that this distinction is too one-sided, and that the discord in men's souls is still more profound and more complex. First of all, the will itself is both free and conditioned. We want what we really do not want, and without any external compulsion we deny ourselves what we really want. Even our most fundamental desires are not quite free. On the other hand, however, our emotional life is not controlled by the same determining laws which control the emotional life of animals. The dismemberment of human nature effected by many philosophers and psychologists is not confirmed by our experience. The spirit is present not only in the intelligence and in the will but also to a certain extent in feelings and emotions. Even in the most primitive and powerful passions there is accordingly a distinct element of freedom. Actions which among animals are entirely pre-determined have among men at least a touch of free initiative. The passions of men are human passions and therefore have a greatness and a worth, and also an element of risk, which we cannot impute to the emotions felt by natural creatures. We are therefore both freer and less free than the early philosophical psychologists believed.

If man had only to be what he in fact is freedom would not be indispensable to him and he could consider it as an extra grace added to his nature, making it possible for him to indulge in a little fantasy. The natural creature, not called upon to perfect itself by its own efforts, has no cause to envy man his freedom. But as man *is* called upon to perfect himself by his own efforts freedom is obviously the distinguishing mark of his nature. Its loss or its betrayal is conducive to a definite ontological decline. Man freely accepts or rejects the call which comes to him from on high to choose the end and purpose of his life. Among all the means he has at his disposal there is not one, however, which could in itself suffice to drive him forward to his freely chosen goal. Neither charitable works nor rosaries nor any other form of prayer can lead him infallibly to God. Only freedom can make these works or prayers the means to an end. If a man finds salvation he does so freely; he is equally free to damn himself. No predestination makes heaven or hell inevitable, and grief, illness, war and other evil occurrences of human life are no more pre-determined than salvation or damnation. Certainly the individual may not have deliberately used his freedom to bring about suffering and war, but because of the mutual dependence of all men an individual's free choice will affect the freedom of others. Only from this point of view can we understand the Christian teaching according to which Adam's free choice had such dire consequences for us all.

A consideration of the fearsome power of human freedom gives superficial thinkers, or men who are oppressed by misfortune, a reason to agree with the philosopher Sartre that freedom is the source and origin of all the miseries of life. Not seldom has man reproached God for having made him free. "Did I beg to be free?" man cries out when he realizes the catastrophe which the use of his freedom may bring about or has already brought about. And indeed it was a very daring thing to entrust the gift of freedom to such a weak and unstable creature as man — yet it is this gift of freedom which makes our life worth living.

*　　*　　*

The most mysterious and insoluble of all the problems relating to human freedom concerns its relation to divine freedom. The conflict between two or more human freedoms is resolved either through a compromise or through the suppression of one by the other. We refer once more to the Hegelian description of the freedom of the master and of that of his slaves. The slaves' freedom is not entirely destroyed but to some extent inhibited by suppression. If the slave submits to these conditions imposed upon him he does so by his free consent, but one day his inhibited freedom may once more assert itself and find expression in revolt, and then it is the master who runs the risk of losing his freedom.

But the relations between God and men must not be understood as similar to those between a master and his slaves. Obviously God's freedom must be absolute. No one and nothing can restrict or impede it. It has nothing to do with determinism and knows no limitations. Everything which in any way exists owes its being and life to divine freedom. Omnipotence is so clearly a characteristic of divine freedom that in the past quite serious theologians did not think it too childish to debate as to whether God can or cannot make a square circle!

In these conditions can human freedom be anything other or more than mere illusion? We believe we choose and act freely, but in reality is it not God alone who chooses and acts through us? For thousands of years philosophers and theologians have meditated on the relationship between God and man. Some have thought that the only way to assert human freedom is to deny absolute freedom to God. Others, whose conception of God is more sublime, refuse to believe in a God who is not absolutely free and so they have to believe that man's freedom is imperfect. Others again, among whom were Jakob Böhm and Nikolai Berdyaev, imagined, for the solution of this difficult problem, a sort of archetypal freedom which preceded both God and man and from which both divine and human freedom are derived. But this thesis also denies the absolute nature of divine freedom.

It seems to us that there is no rational solution of the problem which can fully satisfy the requirements of our spirit. The only valid answer is to be sought on the existential and experimental plane. The Bible describes to us the relationship which God established with men and leaves no room for doubt about the absolute quality of divine freedom. Everything that existed owed its being to God's free will. No natural law, no pre-determination can prevent God from intervening in the course of events. The most immutable natural laws obey him who is both Lord and Law of nature. The innumerable miracles so fully described in the Bible are the visible proofs of the omnipotence of divine freedom.

The same inspired Book, however, tells us that it is not God alone who is free, for he has given freedom also to men, and this is confirmed by our own daily experience. It is moreover clear that human freedom is not merely apparent but authentic: God himself respects it. Instead of compelling us to do what he requires of us he appeals to our freedom of choice and approves our actions and works only in so far as they have their roots in freedom. God asked Abraham, Moses, the Virgin Mary and the apostles for their free consent. What is most difficult to understand and most frightening, but also most sublime, is the fact that human freedom can be turned even against God himself. As the history of Adam, Judas Iscariot and many kings of Juda and Israel shows, the freedom man enjoys enables him to say "no" to God, to reject his appeal, and to frustrate the divine plan for our salvation.

The facts of the absolute freedom of God and the freedom of man form the two principles of truth to which we must hold fast. Nevertheless we must humbly admit that we possess no rational solution to the mystery of freedom. But it is a characteristic of all mysteries not to have a solution: we must be content to make use of the light which enables us to peer a little more closely into their depths.

Although by its nature human freedom is a creative power it can by itself produce chaos, for there is in men's hearts a profound disorder which enables self-confident men to wield a power which is more destructive than creative. Man claims absolute freedom and wishes to liberate himself from all that in any way binds or restricts him: morals, laws and traditions seem to him to be mere obstacles in his path. Of course we also think it desirable that the mature and spiritually minded man should not accept the laws, morals and traditions of his milieu passively under sociological compulsion as a humiliating obligation. Nor must he simply discard them as if they were quite superfluous and incompatible with true freedom. If man yields to the temptation to discard them he will find beyond this social compulsion not absolute freedom but a slavery even worse than that from which he had hoped to get free. In the restless epochs which usually follow wars, revolutions and dictatorships, the craving for freedom over-reaches itself, and then we have not the attainment of true spiritual freedom but a violent descent into anarchy and license. Disorder has the superficial appearance of true freedom, but in fact it drives its victims into the slavery of their unbridled passions and caprices. As man can observe after all revolutions effected in the name of liberty, the unleashing of the forces of freedom leads on the social plane to reigns of terror and to dictatorships which are often even worse than the alleged tyrannies and injustices from which the people had wished to free themselves.

The noblest use which man can make of his freedom is to bring it into perfect conformity and harmony with the will of God. Then the flood of grace will seep down to the deepest roots of our freedom and endow it with the power of truly creative activity. Then morals, traditions and laws will be superseded by liberty and lose their character of social obligations and their power to enslave men. Creative freedom will then find in them a powerful and precious assistance.

Creative freedom, which operates with the help of divine grace, is naturally not satisfied with merely spiritual activity. For an existence committed to time there can be no spiritual freedom without the conquest of sociological freedom. Whether we now have to do with economic, political, moral, intellectual or religious "alienation" (to use Sartre's word) we must always consider this alienation inimical to us personally and inimical to the forward reaching efforts of all men. As my freedom is closely bound up with that of all others it is obviously impossible for me to free myself without contributing to the liberation of my fellow men. Freedom blessed with the creative love of God will naturally differ from the false freedom of license. Our love of true freedom must be strong enough to reject the way which, under the pretense of total liberation, leads to anarchy and the rule of terror.

Freedom, which is not susceptible to spiritual values becomes in the end necessarily destructive and ends in its own ruin. Only a world ruled by the spirit is free from despotism and compulsion. In this temporal sphere in which we have

to spend our lives freedom can reign only when it has succeeded in spiritualizing the world around us. The loving
subordination of human freedom to the freedom of God
does not entail any kind of limitation; it is only in this
way that it can truly grow, because creative power can only
come from God. The claim to autonomy with respect to God
is certainly within the scope of our freedom, but it would inevitably lead to its destruction. People who claim this kind
of autonomy are implicitly supporting the theory of those
philosophers who believe that suicide is the loftiest expression
of human freedom, because they say that by killing himself
a man can show his power not only over the world around
him and over other men but also over his own life. In reality
this is merely deceitful illusion. The most sublime act of
freedom cannot be the destruction of freedom but the fulfillment of the mission entrusted to it.

The conception of freedom is closely bound up with that
of responsibility. For those who deny freedom man is of
course responsible neither for his acts nor for his words, and
not even responsible for his own life. On the other hand,
those who like Sartre believe man to be absolutely free consider him responsible also for all that he is and does and for
all that others are and do — that is, for the whole world, rather
as if he were God. From this point of view he has no excuse: whatever he has done or thought he can only have
done or thought freely, and he is free also in what he
chooses to be. Malraux sees only one chance for men to free
themselves of their oppressive freedom: they can refuse to
live.

As we consider man to be at the same time free and
committed, or conditioned, we cannot agree with either the
determinists or the existentialists. Man is both responsible
and irresponsible. For what he is and does he is responsible
insofar as he is free and acts freely. Certainly, no casuistry
can establish with any precision the degree of freedom of

4

every single action, because it is practically impossible to distinguish clearly between the free element in any act and the element which is psychologically or sociologically predetermined. On the other hand, however, there is always an element of freedom in every human act, and therefore in reality we are to some extent truly responsible for everything. The more authentic our existence the greater and more universal our responsibility naturally becomes.

Everyone of us is responsible not only for himself but for all other people. This is because of the fundamental mutual dependence of all freedoms. Therefore we never have the right to ask with Cain: "Am I my brother's keeper?" We are even responsible for the whole world because it cannot achieve its final end without us. No one and nothing is empowered to release us from this mutual obligation. The greatness and worth of men are based on their freedom and responsibility.

The notion of responsibility, which is firmly and universally established in the conscience of men, presupposes something transcendent, which is greater than man himself and to which he feels he is called to render an account. There is no sense in claiming that man is responsible to himself alone. Every conception of the world as totally self-sufficient is in danger of rejecting all notions of responsibility, even if, like the existentialists, we talk endlessly about the individual's general and total responsibility. In some cases our family, our native land or a lofty humanistic or scientific ideal may usurp the role of this necessary transcendental element, but God alone reveals what is truly transcendent. From him we receive freedom and the commission which we must obey through our own free activity. We must render him an account of what we have done with our freedom, and therefore we are responsible to him for everyone and everything.

CHAPTER VI

ADVENTURE AND CHOICE

It is possible for us to have a burning desire to follow our true calling and to enter into all the wealth which freedom can give us, and yet to find ourselves in a situation which is by no means simple or pleasant. As soon as we begin to understand our real condition in this world we become aware of innumerable possibilities opening out before us. No predestined route is already there for us to discover and to follow. We must hew our own way in the unknown primeval jungle, and this way may be in one of a thousand different directions. As long as our earthly and temporal life lasts we can express our freedom only through innumerable choices and decisions.

It is not a case of a single choice which a man makes once and for all and which then binds him in life and in eternity. According to the theologians, the angels made such a final choice at the very moment of their creation. But human nature has nothing of this angelic simplicity. Psychological analysis reveals the complexity of our innermost being: a multiplicity which nevertheless tries to form a unity. Moreover, man is immersed in time and space and both of these are even more complex than he is. According to the laws which govern the multiplicity which tries to achieve unity we are therefore bound to make the inevitable decisions, not once and for all but continually, until the last moment of our earthly existence. In every moment we have to choose between the various goals which life sets before us, every one of which has its own particular beauty and value. Even when a man chooses as his life's goal a vocation as important as the service of God or of his country or the advancement of progress for all mankind, it is still impossible for him to abide tranquilly by this decision, once he has made it. For other goals are continually presenting themselves, in competition with those already chosen, and they force him either to question his earlier choice or to persevere in it with renewed ardor. We must also in every moment choose among the innumerable means which may help us to reach our chosen end.

In order to withdraw from the hazards of making a decision, would it not be possible to set one's face against making any kind of choice? In theory this may be possible, but in practice we can only reject one alternative by choosing another. The determined rejection of any choice is already a decision, and this decision not to make a choice deprives us of the power to control our own destiny and leaves us the passive plaything of fate.

* * *

Many of our contemporaries feel a strong aversion to making any existential choice. The timid lack the courage required for any important decision. Every choice implies a commitment, with consequences which may not be foreseen. Man is fundamentally a complex creature and all his faculties are interdependent. Because he chooses this particular woman and not another he gives a certain direction not only to his married life but also in practice to the whole of his life on earth and perhaps even to his life in eternity. Other people too may be more or less directly affected by this highly personal choice and this effect may even last for many generations. For example, if Hitler's father had not chosen that particular woman for his wife but another woman instead, perhaps there would have been no National Socialism, no second World War, and the present world situation would have been very different. The same thing often applies to the choice of a job, a political party, a trade union or a philosophical or religious concept of the world. More or less obviously, and in varying degrees, every one of these decisions may assign to our future actions and even to our whole lives a certain direction and purpose.

If only it were possible to know beforehand all the consequences of our choice! But this is quite impossible. However long and carefully a man may reflect before he makes a decision, however attentively he examines every aspect of his choice, the unforeseeable and unforeseen element is still so great that every choice is frought with danger. Suppose a young man marries a girl who is beautiful as well as rich. How can he know beforehand that his father-in-law will soon go bankrupt or that an accident will mar his wife's beauty? If he chooses the profession of an electrical engineer it is hardly possible to predict the future prospects of this industry. A certain political party is today all-powerful and offers the brightest opportunities for a brilliant career to any ambitious man, but the political situation may change and the members of this party may be molested or even persecuted.

Are we well aware of the risks incurred in every important decision? If we are we need much courage to make it. The timid, who do not succeed in overcoming their fear, shy away from this obligation of making a choice. They remain in a constant state of hesitation, petrified at the thought of an impending decision.

But the circumstances of their lives often compel them willy-nilly to make a choice, and they may chance to choose well. Nevertheless, they will soon be questioning their choice again, regretting ever having made it, and trying to get free of it. But when they thus refuse to make binding decisions they condemn themselves to submitting passively to an unreal, lusterless existence. They may perhaps dream of a more real life, and even admire it, but they will never live it themselves.

The timid man is, however, not the only one to shun the duty of making a decision. The egoist finds it just as unpleasant, or even more unpleasant, although for quite different reasons. Every choice, as we have already said, presupposes the existence of several solutions, the possibility of choosing between different actions. It is therefore inevitable that when a man chooses one of these possibilities he must renounce all the others. In some circumstances this renunciation may be extremely painful. A young man who decides to become a priest renounces *ipso facto* the joys of family life, so dear to men's hearts, and the innumerable possibilities of activity and development which a lay condition offers. When a man marries one woman he gives up the thought of all others, even of the *grande passion* which he may one day experience. The fear of having to make such a sacrifice is the reason why the "heroes" of the novels of Gide and Sartre try to avoid making the final existential choice, or at least to defer it as long as possible.

To all appearances the superficial man who sacrifices nothing enjoys the greatest freedom. But in reality he is no freer than the timid soul of whom we have already spoken. He believes—or at least he acts as if he believed—that the refusal to make the sacrifice or renunciation necessitated by a definite choice has made him a superman, capable of great deeds. He does not know that it is precisely these successive choices, often concerned with quite small things and all requiring sacrifices and renunciations, which eventually make men able to do great things. Despite their claim to be Supermen, the egoistic, easy-going and self-indulgent are really Sub-men incapable of living real lives.

Fortunately, most of us are neither too superficial nor too timid to recognize the necessity of choice: we do not from the very start refuse to make personal decisions. Generally, however, we are content to make the small, circumscribed decisions of everyday. We say that life has taught us to be prudent. The absolutely decisive choice which could commit our whole lives seems to us not only unnecessary but very dangerous for it would be extremely difficult to draw back from such an absolute commitment. It might lead us too far, induce us to do all sorts of foolish things, and ruin our peace of mind.

The philosopher Hegel was the exponent of the relativity of all things and all values, and for this reason Kierkegaard called his philosophy one of "contemptible mediocrity." It is particularly opposed to any truly final choice which could profoundly affect our own lives and those of others. According to Hegel no value exists which deserves or justifies such total commitment. Certainly he too spoke of absolute truth and absolute values but these were for him ideal conceptions which bore no relation to the actual lives of people in this world, in which everything is only "to a certain extent" true and good. It would, of course, be foolish to bind oneself by an absolute decision to anything merely relative. And, as everything is only "relatively" true and good so nothing is wholly false or evil. Total renunciation is therefore wrong and impossible, for everything contains "some good." Consequently we dare not totally reject anything, just as we must not totally dedicate ourselves to anything.

It is not difficult to recognize in this Hegelian thesis the

"philosophy" by the light of which many of our contemporaries, of all social classes, live their daily lives. It is clear that
such a conception of the world, if it became a principle of
human conduct, would permit only a very mediocre kind of
existence. Kierkegaard was therefore right to oppose it so
sternly, although we must not blame Hegel alone for the
dreadful mediocrity of the lives of so many of our contemporaries: other philosophies and various other un-philosoph-
ical factors too have played their part.

* * *

To make an absolute choice is a necessity for all who do
not intend to be content with mediocrity, who seek all that is
great and true and wish to live intensely. Such a choice contains in itself the explicit intention of never going back on
it, of being faithful to it forever. We know that this decision
will commit our whole life, and possibly our eternal life too,
and we consent to this. As it is impossible to know all its consequences beforehand such a choice requires great daring.

So once more we face the question: is such a decision
overbold and therefore wrong? Our answer is: it is permissible
only on condition that one is convinced that there exist values
which are good and true not only "to a certain extent." If we
choose these values it is because we have learned from experience that they are absolutely good and true. And if we
categorically reject them it is because we have no hesitation
in judging them to be absolutely false and evil. It is clear
that not all values can be the object of an absolute choice or
of an absolute rejection. Only what is, in itself, absolute, or
what we consider to be absolute, can justify such a binding
decision.

Religion, which in the truest sense of the word means
the relation between God and man, is of all good things that
which has most right to claim our absolute commitment. We

fully agree with Kierkegaard who writes: "Men have said many strange, pitiable and reprehensible things about Christianity, but the most foolish thing ever said about it is that it is true 'to a certain extent.'" It is enough to open the Old or the New Testament to see that God, under both the Old and the New Covenants, required from man an absolute unconditional allegiance: "I am the Lord your God...you shall have no other gods....I am your God and you are my people....Thou shalt love the Lord thy God with all thy heart...." This is the dominant theme of the Old Testament. Any conditional allegiance, any compromise with other gods and other worship, is looked upon by Jehovah as a personal affront which must be most severely punished. The "meek" Christ of the Gospel is hardly less stern: "No man can serve two masters....Sell all that you have...and follow me.... Whoever loves his father and mother more than he loves me is not worthy to be my disciple....You have heard...but I say to you." And Jesus himself chose to drink to the dregs the chalice which the Father had appointed for him to drink, and to love men unto death on the Cross.

Such an absolute choice must still be made today by all who wish to bear the name of Christ. There is no place for conditional allegiance in the Christian life. A man like Nietzsche, who scorned and rejected Christianity with all its dogmas and morality, is perhaps more true to the logic of the Gospels than some so-called practicing Christians, many of whom have not made an absolute decision for God and are prepared to accept the Gospel only "up to a certain point." Some see Jesus only as loving and mild, and are enchanted with the "poetry" of his life, charmed by this "fine preacher of fair Galilee," as the famous apostate Ernest Renan described him. Other, more serious, people appreciate his moral teaching but usually only insofar as it does not disturb their slothful ease. Others again look to the Gospel for cheap emotionalism, and so on. But all think it necessary to select from the Lord's precepts, parables and teachings those passages which seem to them to fit their own case. Whatever conflicts with their own prejudices and comforts they call "metaphor" or "oriental exaggeration." They do their best to ignore what has been called the "folly of the Gospel." A young Christian woman I know, who has read the Gospel many times, believes that it contains merely teachings about human joy and free self-expression. When her friends tried to convince her that the Cross occupies a very important place in the religion of Christ she got very angry and broke off all connection with her Group, because she was more or less aware that this interpretation could lead her further than she wished to go. Even more numerous, especially in "pious" circles, are those who see only the gloomy aspect of this same religion. Life with Christ means for them a perpetual Good Friday; they are always in mourning and shocked when they see gay and happy people in church. They seem to have quite forgotten that Christ is risen to die no more, and that the world is intended to be not a vale of tears but the site for the building of God's kingdom.

The same Christ died on the Cross, rose again and now reigns in his Father's house. The same Jesus of Nazareth who was the friend of sinners and shocked the pious folk of his time by his loving patience with the adulteress, made very stern claims on his disciples and followers with regard to honesty and chastity. He preached meekness and resignation to the poor but condemned the ungodly rich and the miserly. He made the hunger and thirst after righteousness the cornerstone of his Church.

We cannot accept literally his words to the poor while we treat his condemnation of the ungodly rich as mere "oriental exaggeration." We must either accept all or refuse all: what is absolute cannot be divided.

Here is not the place to speak about the "Freethinkers" who accept only the moral teaching of the Gospel, or about the aesthetes who are enraptured with its "poetry," but who refuse to consider it the word of God. I welcome these "sympathizers" less warmly than the openly hostile men like Sartre who declare there is no God and that therefore nothing has any meaning or eternal value. Christ says "yes" and "no" but never "perhaps." Those who frankly say "no" are often nearer to his "yes" than those who say both "yes" and "no" at the same time.

It is by no means our intention to belittle the courage required to make every deliberate choice. It is often possible to confuse idolatry with the worship of God. Because they have not discovered the real Absolute, many brave men, who rejected any thought of conditional allegiance or of mediocrity, come to believe that their race, or their country, or their party or some other human good has absolute value. But once they have freed themselves by choosing what is truly absolute they will see that the choice of less true values leads to individual or collective disaster. Most of the tragic occurrences which have marked our own era have originated in some form of idolatry. The disillusionments which are the inevitable result of these mistaken devotions are the reason why many of our contemporaries refuse to risk making any choice. They have not yet recognized the enormous difference that exists between the worship of God and idolatry.

But on the psychological plane it is indisputable that a man who has dared to make a binding choice, even if it concerns some merely relative good, is nearer to the real Absolute than the man who is a slave to relativist theories or the superficial thinker; both these refuse to make any binding choice and are always trying to protect their own "independence." The man who insists on choosing what is a merely relative good has certainly more chance of contributing to the improvement of individual and collective life than the man who chooses something which has absolute value but who is not prepared to abide by his choice unconditionally.

However important the choice of the Absolute may be for

the fulfillment of our life's purpose, it is still not the only choice we have to make. As long as we live innumerable other decisions are thrust upon us. Some of them are, in their nature and significance very similar to an absolute choice. One might indeed describe them as *relative-absolutes,* if such a combination of words were permissible, or rather as *near-absolutes.* Other decisions, which have to be made frequently throughout our lives, are in themselves less significant; they have nothing absolute about them and are therefore entirely relative.

The first, and perhaps the most important *near-absolute* choice which everyone must make is the choice which concerns his own personality. A man is born in a certain country, or a certain milieu, within a certain social class. He has inherited some particular qualities and failings, and therefore has already a particular character and temperament. At the start these must be considered as pre-determined, as things which are imposed upon him without his freedom of choice being in any way involved. They are factors which form his basic disposition, with which he has to reckon in all circumstances. But he must not submit passively to this pre-determined disposition. He has the capacity and the duty to react against it and so to exercise a definite choice with relation to it: a man can decide either for or against his disposition.

To react against it means rejecting it because he does not consider it sufficiently "interesting" or because he has not the courage to come to terms with it. It is however a grave illusion to believe that a man may discard it completely. By rejecting it he condemns his life to total sterility. Instead of controlling and perfecting his disposition he will have to suffer it and submit to it. Many highly gifted men have accomplished nothing positive, and have disappointed the expectations placed in them, simply because they have refused to acknowledge the fundamental elements of their character. One man finds the mentality and tendencies of the era in which he lives incompatible with his own ideas. He may be a Christian living in a pagan epoch, or he may be actuated by moral principles in a milieu in which immorality flourishes; or he may have the making of an artisan but be obliged to live in an industrialized society. Therefore he refuses to come to terms with his own era or to acknowledge it in any positive way. Spiritually he still lives in "the good old times," which are long past. He compares the people, morals and prices of his own day with those of pre-war days, or of the Middle Ages, or of early Christian times. In order to convince himself that he is "doing something" he joins anachronistic groups and movements, calls out "Long live the King" or "Heil Hitler," although he knows very well that there is no longer a king and that Hitler died many years ago.

What positive results can he obtain from this sort of deliberate disassociation from his own epoch? Certainly such a negative attitude to reality will not change or improve the atheism or the immorality or the industrialization, or even the government of his day. Instead of exerting any influence over these he abandons them to their own dynamic, and in one way or another he will have to suffer in his own person the negative influence of his own times. In this way the French Catholics were for more than a hundred years completely ineffective in politics because most of them, and the most influential among them, categorically refused to come to terms with their own epoch. They pined for the "good old days" of the monarchy, the old family customs and the old conditions for working people, and so they lost any chance of bringing a Christian influence to bear upon the actual situation before them.

On a more personal plane there are also many people who will not admit the real facts about themselves. They invent for themselves ancestors and refuse to admit the faults and weaknesses of their own characters and temperaments, and they over estimate their spiritual and physical capacities. Instead of integrating themselves with their milieu they consciously or unconsciously play the part of the "misunderstood." They envy everyone who belongs to a higher social class and always feel resentful. This causes the weakening, or even the loss, of the dynamic force of their personality. As long as they refuse to come face to face with themselves they have no chance of living real lives.

The individual and psychological gifts of nature and external sociological circumstances will only be truly human, effective and fruitful when we by our own free choice transform them all by integrating them in our own actual existential life. By freely accepting them we absorb them into our own dynamic personalities. As long as human nature seems to us an unavoidable fate it can only be an obstacle to us, or the source of constant discouragement. But when by our own free choice we come to terms with our own natures then freedom assumes control, loosens the bonds of determinism and gives nature her share in creative activity. From the moment when man positively understands his own times and his own country, his personal character and his past, in short, his whole human condition, he will no longer feel all this to be a heavy burden that has been laid upon his shoulders by some external power. The duality between "myself" and "my body" or "my nature," will cease: spirit and body will be united in the whole self. Because of our free choice our bodies which seem to be alien to our "true being" will then be truly ourselves: we shall have chosen ourselves. After choosing myself in this way I shall no longer be an author living in Paris in the twentieth century — as Plato says the soul lives in the body "like the sailor in the ship"— but I shall live as a twentieth century man and author. Through choosing to be myself I take to myself all the greatness and all the misery of my own century and become its spokesman.

It would be mistaken to believe that a man condemns himself to a fatalistic and ineffectual attitude to life when he chooses himself as he really is. In spite of all appearances the contrary is true. Through this choice he obtains the means and the power to fulfill his own mission in life. As we said in our first chapter, a man does not magically produce out of nothing the material with which he must build his life: the external and internal elements which form his nature provide all the material he requires. Nothing solid and permanent can be built on an imaginary foundation. While a man is choosing himself, in his own epoch and his own land, in his own total existential situation, he is at the same time acquiring the power to influence his epoch and his country, his character and his environment. But, although choosing his real self does not mean that he willingly consents to follow all the trends and fashions of his time and his country; he can only prove his mastery of the current by throwing himself into it.

The existential choice of the real self is seen in practice to be much harder than it appears at first. Only painfully and by means of constant and persevering effort can it be achieved. It is a long and hard struggle against all those obstacles of which we have already spoken, which stand in the way of our conquest of freedom. We must also be prepared for many failures. Like any other choice, the choice of one's real self cannot be made without sacrifice and self-denial. We must be prepared to do some cutting down to size and some streamlining if we wish to see ourselves as we really are. In order to be someone or something we must give up trying to be everything. But it often happens that self-betrayal and artificiality have become so much a part of our nature that we cannot forgo them without much grief and heartache. The inevitable limitations which the choice of our true self imposes upon us apparently hamper the legitimate desire to expand which is especially strong among us today. Nearly all of us believe that in order to expand and live intensively we should not only possess all things but be all things too. If we tell a child to choose between two toys he will most probably answer: "I want both." The primitive man and the superficial hedonist (psychologically, the latter can hardly be distinguished from the former, although he is often more highly educated) often behave like children. They are afraid of choosing because they fear the limitations which this choice will entail. The dilettante and the more sophisticated eclectic can never experience the exuberant joyfulness which proceeds from the daring choice of the true self. They can only live humdrum or dissipated lives.

When a man has chosen his true self he must try to build, upon this foundation, what he will and must become. This task is so important, for a man's own vocation as well as for the creative work of the world in general, that it may not be left to caprice or chance. Like good architects we have to prepare a scheme to serve as our ground-plan. This ground-plan guides us in our choice of the working ideals of our life. The choice of our life's aim, of our ground-plan, will condition all the particular and successive choices which life will set before us.

The choice of our situation in life is the most typical choice of a ground-plan, provided, of course, that this situation is sought not only as a means of livelihood or as a social career but as our vocation in this temporal world. When a man accepts the love of a woman, when he becomes a doctor, engineer, soldier or priest, a Jesuit or a Franciscan, he must always make a choice which we may describe as *near-absolute*. It is not for him lightly to question this choice once it is made — only important and relevant motives could justify him in reconsidering it. The particular choices he will make after this initial tracing of a ground-plan — whether they concern his studies, his home, or other interests — will always be conditioned by this first decision.

The superficial hedonist may find the choice of his life's ideal even more unpleasant, if that were possible, than the choice of his true self. He would still like to enjoy all the flowers, titbits and luxuries of life, but he knows that some of these are incompatible with his original ground-plan.

* * *

All eminent men, all those who have played a positive role in the history of mankind, lived wholeheartedly for one great ideal. This is true, of course, in the first place of Christ but it is also true of Socrates, Napoleon, Marx, Pasteur, Gandhi and Einstein. However numerous and varied the deeds and words of Christ were, they showed no lack of an underlying consistency: all were directed to the glorification of the Father. Socrates was interested only in the discovery of the truth. Therefore the choice of a life purpose is the most essential element in the dynamic condition of all who live real lives, and they draw from it their strength, the concentration of energies which is unknown to the ordinary man. Without the choice of a life purpose it would have been impossible for them to become "great men" and do great things.

Naturally we are not expected to despise all the other good things of life but to see that these find their proper place and significance within our life purpose. The statesman whose fundamental ideal has been service to his country but who does not try to integrate his patriotism in a love for all mankind, will become a malicious and chauvinistic fanatic, such as we have seen at the head of more than one totalitarian state. Certainly the absolute choice of a fundamental ground-plan gives the chauvinist his powerful working strength, but fanaticism blinds him so much that he cannot see the innumerable ties which unite his own country to others. It is very hard for him to avoid suffering from the delusion of greatness, and so finally bringing about disaster, not only for other peoples but also for his own beloved native land.

A Christian who denies all the beauty in "profane" poetry

and art, the truth present in non-Christian philosophies and the religious element in pagan worship, will undoubtedly be a very poor follower of Christ, and we know from experience that such fanatical Christians end as heretics.

The truly mature man loves one great ideal only and serves this. But in the light of this ideal he also loves all that is good, true and beautiful, and serves these wherever he finds them. I am reminded of the martyr Justin, one of the early philosophers, who was converted to Christianity in the second century. He reverenced the beauty of Greek statues and found in these masterpieces by pagan sculptors new cause for praising God. Of course this holy saint loved God above all else — in fact we may say he loved nothing else, but out of his love for God he found the strength and the motive to love all men and all creatures most devotedly. Moreover, his passionate love for creatures helped him to love his Creator even more. In the life of Francis of Assisi Christ was indeed all and everything, but who could see in his passionate love of Christ the slightest trace of fanaticism or narrow-mindedness? Who has not heard of his equally tender love for all his "little brothers," people, animals, the birds of the air, the sun, water and the earth itself?

The main purpose of the existential choice is to help men to lift themselves above the life which is dissipated by temporal and worldly cares to the one true life — from which is expansion to a life which gathers itself together for future action.

CHAPTER VII

AVAILABILITY AND READINESS

We have already pointed out that there are many people, especially in the educated and cultured classes, who are not eager to give a definite direction to their lives by making an absolute choice. They are afraid of putting themselves into a sort of spiritual straitjacket or of becoming narrow-minded fanatical exponents of a party, a sect, a book or an idea.

They wish to remain open-minded and ready for all possible and impossible contingencies; they wish to leave the door open to all possible enjoyments, and they hope that this way they will be able to avoid the complications of life, or at least to simplify them. Their ambition is to be ready for any sudden call or any eventuality. In their opinion availability and commitment are mutually exclusive terms. They prefer the possibility to the accomplishment, and are more interested in the chase than in the booty. In their opinion anyone who has, for example, chosen the Catholic faith is no longer free to accept any spiritual enrichment offered by any other religion. One who has chosen the communist part will, for example, no longer listen to the teaching of Christian social movements about the solution of the problem of the proletariat. To pledge one's word to a woman or to a friend robs one of the chance of meeting an even more suitable wife, or a better friend.

Here readiness and availability are seen as total passivity, mere expectation. In order to remain uncommitted one must be willing to consent to all possibilities and accept all trends of thought, but without ever pledging allegiance to any. One must pay great attention to all one's emotional impulses, impressions and desires. When one acts — and how can all action be avoided? — one should do so as far as possible without a reason or motive, for it is only unmotivated action which does not commit a man, and so does not tie him down.

Such a concept of open-mindedness is obviously incompatible with any hope of forming a relationship with the Absolute. People who claim to preserve this sort of availability condemn themselves to total inaction and become parasites living on human society. Obviously those who strive to live real lives will reject that sort of passivity. If there were no other possible way of preserving one's availability one could hardly condemn those who prefer to foreshorten their spiritual horizons and forego most possibilities of developing their own personalities, rather than become like a length of empty rubber tubing.

Fortunately, true living by no means implies narrow and restricted lives. It is possible to live a fully committed life and yet at the same time keep an open mind. Open-mindedness itself may become an active way of life instead of being a passive obstacle to true living, and so it can strengthen the existential reality of life.

Like all other created and finite beings, man is not a "whole" which has reached perfection by its own efforts and looks upon all the other creatures of the world as so many means appointed to serve it. As we have already seen, a man does not make his fundamental choice merely in relation to himself, and his freedom is not intended primarily to further the assertion and expansion of his own selfish craving for power. He also is a member of a "hierarchy of creatures" and, as a creature, belongs to human society. There is in our world no single creature to whom it has been given to fulfill its life purpose or calling in any other way but through the acceptance of the function allotted to it, in relation to all other members of the human — or even of the cosmic — community. The whole vocation of members of the lower ranks in the hierarchy seems to consist simply in faithfully fulfilling the function entrusted to them in relation to the higher ranks of created beings. For a man, because of his double nature, things are much more complex.

He has, first of all, a very definite role to play in relation to all the lower creatures, that is, all natural creatures. This role does not consist merely in making use of them but consists just as much, and even more, in the obligation to serve them. We have already seen that nature can achieve her desired end, her meaning, justification and final purpose, through man's mediation. He has no right to decline to play this intermediary role because, for example, he despises nature. He may not treat her as if she were of no importance. His attitude towards her must be that of a magnanimous ruler who sees all his underlings as faithful friends, for whom he is responsible to God. However small and insignificant natural creatures may seem in themselves to be, man must feel the greatest respect for them all. Certainly Francis of Assisi, who loved all creatures as brothers and sisters, should serve as a noble example, but his example must be integrated with that of Teilhard de Chardin who was not content to observe the universe with loving admiration but spent his whole life trying to reveal its mysteries, to further the purposes of its evolution and to spiritualize it.

Of particular importance, however, is the mission which

every man has to fulfill with regard to other men. We can never sufficiently emphasize the fundamental solidarity of all people and the interdependence of their vocations. Everyone of us must consider it a duty to feel truly responsible for everyone else, and everyone has been entrusted with the task of helping all his brother men to rise higher. Above all, no human creature must be considered or used as a mere tool in the service of any cause. However sublime a cause may be, it can never be greater than man himself, who is made in the likeness of God. All men are members of the same community of the builders of God's kingdom. Not through the efforts of individuals, however heroic they may be, will this kingdom be built, but through the common efforts of all men. The final result depends in the first place, therefore, on the solidarity and strength of this community. No individual person must be thought of as insignificant or useless for the fulfillment of mankind's purpose. In every "man in the street" we must recognize a brother whom we need and who has need of us. This is no mere sentimental illusion but a profound psychological and ontological certainty.

But, apart from all this, human life has an important function to fulfill in relation to God. He is the "whole," whom all individual creatures acknowledge. In a certain sense we are this function and nothing else, and we live truly only insofar as we fulfill it. We are God's servants, not only by our desire but because of our metaphysical nature. All our actions are so many means to enable us to give him more perfect service. And this service means that we are co-laborers with God in his own work.

None of these three functions, or rather none of these three aspects of the only true human function in this world, is incidental or an extra something added to the already perfect natural world. They are in the very nature of man: every wish and every attempt to separate them debases life to a sub-human condition, removes it from the order to which it belongs and finally robs it of any possibility of being human in the full sense of the word. Man plays his part within the cosmic whole and is a good and faithful servant of the whole insofar as he places himself, to the extent of his power, at the disposal of all natural creatures, of his brother men and of God. In the active fulfillment of his function, and in the acceptance of all other creatures, is real availability to be found.

The man who refuses to commit himself may easily be recognized because he considers himself the center and culminating point of his world. Nothing can move him or hold his attention, except his own person and his own problems. The only conversation which he finds enthralling is about himself, his health, his family and possessions, his business and occupations. He has a very highly developed love of possessions and an acute awareness of his own rights. If he belongs to a church and believes in God, it is always *his* God and *his* salvation which matter. It is hard for him to admit in all honesty that his God is also everyone else's, and that God's main task is not to watch over his particular selfish interests. If his affairs go ill and those of his neighbor go well he accuses God of injustice and hints at feeling doubts about his faith.

Other men are, practically speaking, of no importance in the psychological "make-up" of the man who refuses to become involved. He considers the people he meets as obstacles to be overcome or as means to be used for his own selfish purposes. As he thinks of nothing else but himself he cannot see himself in relation to others: for him all others exist only in relation to himself. The spirit of service is not in him. He generally thinks of himself as a superman to whom all is permitted and whom all other men should serve. He is distrustful, forever afraid of being robbed of any of his alleged rights. He acknowledges obligations only to himself and clings jealously to all his possessions — wealth, friends, ideas and prejudices — trembling with fear at the thought of losing any of them. Sometimes he thinks he is a happy man, but in reality unhappiness is the normal condition of his life, the normal state of his conscience. The beauties of nature rarely move him because even in these he can only see objects to be made use of, and he never tries to discern any spiritual bond with nature. He thinks he has everything, but as he has severed all transcendental links with other creatures, he is more possessed than possessing.

This description of the man who is closed and unresponsive to his fellows helps us to understand the psychology of that other man who is open-minded and responsive, and who, even if rich in earthly goods, has not the spirit of possessions but the spirit of poverty. He does not look upon natural creatures — and still less on other men — as if he had rights over them, but rather looks upon himself as one belonging to all others. He does not dare to think even of himself as his own possession, or as something upon which he can impose his arbitrary will, for he is conscious that, with all he is and has, he is enrolled in the service of a higher cause. His customary attitude is one of waiting to be called upon, and this call may come from the world, or from other people, or from God.

Despite superficial appearances there is no element of passivity in this readiness and responsiveness. Neither God nor man, nor the world itself, wants us to be passive: they want us to cooperate with them actively. They expect from us creative initiative, free choice, persevering fidelity and involvement. Therefore, instead of being in opposition to a free choice, involvement shows itself to be the necessary condition for making it. In fact, true living demands a certain forgetfulness of self, the subordination of an individual's interests to the interests of others and of society as a whole, and liberation from what one is and has. But all this is possible only to the man who is open and responsive to his fellow men.

If one single choice were to determine the course of our life once and for all, then anyone who had already made it would no longer be capable of other choices. One would be free only up to the moment of making this final choice, but never again. The committed man would therefore be no more open to other choices than the man who refused to commit himself. But we know that in human life every individual decision is usually but the preparation for new and more difficult decisions to come, and that fidelity to certain commitments demands that we should commit ourselves still further. After every decision and every commitment we must therefore hold ourselves ready for new choices and new involvements.

Naturally, it is not a question of holding ourselves in readiness for every conceivable eventuality, for this would result in no final commitment and we should be consenting to that superficial concept of readiness which, at the beginning of this chapter, we categorically rejected as incompatible with the idea of true living. We must be responsive only to those appeals which oblige us, within the limits of our personal ,vocation, to rise to higher things. As we have said, readiness makes choice possible, especially the choice which commits one's whole life and which necessarily entails painful renunciations and is possible only to those who do not seek merely their own good. It is nevertheless indisputable that every absolute choice increases our availability.

The man who is responsive and receptive is neither narrow-minded nor hard-hearted; he is not imprisoned in systems and prejudices. Naturally, in accordance with the life's ideal he has chosen, he has his own notions and convictions about many things. Nevertheless he will not forget that even the most sublime human intelligence will never be able to embrace the totality of truth, and will therefore always be liable to err. He freely admits that in all probability there are aspects of truth which he has not yet grasped in their entirety, and that therefore the person who contradicts him may perhaps have discovered a different aspect of the same truth. It would therefore be worthwhile for him to listen to him attentively, in order to try to understand the other man's point of view and so learn something from him. In my teacher and friend, the world famous palaeontologist Teilhard de Chardin, this conviction was so strong that he felt able to assert that scientific truth was only attainable through the common efforts of a group, because even the most brilliant individual thinker is liable to err a thousand times more frequently than the average "working committee." Such spiritual receptivity does not, however, lead to a philosophy of relativity. In intellectual discussions, although I adhere to my own principles I am always ready to enrich these with those crumbs of truth which may be found in even the most erroneous beliefs.

The open-hearted man is convinced of his own poverty and of his need for constant intellectual development, and for this very reason he has a creative power which is in direct proportion to his accessibility. He is responsive to God's influence and at all times ready to work with him. In this readiness lies the secret of his effective action.

As the open-minded man does not ascribe his successes and conquests exclusively to his own merits, even failures will have no power to discourage him. He is always ready to start afresh and to enjoy new experiences. He is not afraid to face a challenge. I know an old Christian "Activist" who was from his youth up convinced of the spiritual and social value of joint enterprise in industry and agriculture and who himself built up several thriving concerns in the course of about thirty years. However, for various reasons, over which he had no control, these enterprises all foundered, so that he lost not only his own wealth but also the money invested in them by several of his relatives and friends. Another man might have given up in despair and become embittered. But as, in all his endeavors, he had sought no advancement for himself but only the fulfillment of what he held to be his vocation, he did not allow his misfortunes to discourage him. After the last world war he started a new and important joint enterprise and this time, the external conditions being favorable, his success was complete. In success as in failure this man's enthusiasm and optimism were unaltered.

*   *   *

At peace with God, dedicated to the service of all his fellows and responsive to the beauties of nature, the open-minded man is naturally happy. The less one thinks about oneself the less one fears to be misjudged or scorned.

In the present state of human nature readiness is not usually spontaneous, for sin and selfishness are practically synonymous. Certainly, if readiness required no effort we should all be ready and approachable, but since it means active expectation and participation, many of us are unwilling to become really available. It costs fatigue and effort to emerge from one's egocentricity and to accept other people not as objects to dispose of at our will but as people with individual vocations. Obviously we may expect help and service from others, but we must always be ready to serve them too.

Although it is not easy, in the midst of all our commitments, to avoid sterile dissipation and fanaticism, yet in this avoidance lies the foundation of true availability and readiness. Generally speaking, all choices and commitments tend to concentrate a man's energies as forcefully as possible on the task he has undertaken, so that anything which lies beyond this task loses its interest and appeal. It often happens that a man who has never seemed selfish can speak of nothing but his own work, his political party or his art, once he has made his fundamental choice and set himself to serve a great cause. He appears to have become totally impervious. Since he has misinterpreted the true nature of existential readiness he is afraid to weaken the strength of his commitment by trying to remain open and responsive to other claims. His irresponsiveness is motivated by his fear of slipping into a superficial relativism.

Let us therefore insist once more that true availability does not mean superficiality and a dissipation of energies, but is always the fruit of effort. This effort may prove easier for one man than for another, but it is possible and necessary for all. On the one hand readiness makes a choice possible, and on the other hand readiness is in itself a choice. We must choose in order to be always ready to make the next choice.

* * *

A man can seldom find an easy and peaceful way of development. Nearly all need another person or some particular occurrence to shake them out of their "natural" selfishness. The walls within which we are imprisoned must be broken down in order that we may see the vulnerability and foolishness of the individual who thinks he is the center of the whole world. The example of men who show a spirit of exceptional or even of heroic enterprise helps us to desire and to attain the same degree of readiness which they possessed. But the revelation of love or friendship or the beauty of nature is also a means of setting us on the right path. When the day comes on which a man is capable of admiring something or someone other than himself, he will have taken the first step in the direction of availability. Then he will understand that others too are on the same road, that he may and must receive spiritual assistance from them, that he must not use them selfishly as his tools but must respect their freedoms as well as his own. As long as we strive only for our own advancement, our availability will remain imperfect, and we shall not succeed in overcoming our egoism. True liberation from the bonds of egocentricity will come only when a man who, through admiration for another person or for something else, has become responsive and hears the call to place himself in the service of a cause which is greater than himself. This may be some altruistic human ideal which friends and circumstances have revealed to him. If he does not see in this ideal merely a means of furthering his own purposes but instead shows even a trace of true self-forgetfulness and undertakes a task without a selfish purpose, then this man is truly on the way to becoming perfectly available.

Even a passionate human attachment can arouse total devotion to the beloved person. At the beginning, this readiness to give seems only to exist in relation to the beloved, but if the love is true then there is a very good chance that it may open a man's heart to all other people too and to the whole world. There are also many other unusual circumstances — war, imprisonment, disasters, etc.— which may draw the individual out of his selfishness and enable him to discover the brotherhood of all men, without expecting any reward or personal advantage. We have known occasions when such a sudden conversion has made a man ready and available, even to a truly heroic degree.

Perfect readiness apparently belongs only to the saints. They have renounced all possessions, even the possession of themselves and of their world. Without any diminishment of themselves they have entered the service not merely of a person or of a great ideal but of God himself. But while they give themselves to God and submit to him they are ready, with him and in him, to accept all other people and the whole world and to place themselves at their service. In them one can see the greatest harmony between total commitment and perfect availability, and for this reason their lives, although generally modest and unknown, have such extraordinary significance in the history of the world.

CHAPTER VIII

COMMITMENT

We have already said that human freedom is acquired by means of many different and successive choices. In this way a man accepts his own life, together with his past and his vocation. But the existential choice is no interim inconsequential act from which he could free himself if he so desired. It normally leads to a commitment, to a special mission in the struggle for existence.

True commitment only exists with regard to people, and practically never with regard to things. If I have chosen an apple for dessert I do not feel in any way committed to it. I may even reject it and set it aside without any objective reason, and choose another fruit. Certain things may well deputize, as it were, for actual persons, but even then one does not commit oneself to the things themselves but to the people for whom they stand. But every time a choice links us directly or indirectly with a person the result is an existential bond which unites us with this person. It must however be observed that the commitment is not something added to the choice, like a second action, but is included in the choice: we choose and commit ourselves in the same action. According to the nature of our choice we pledge ourselves to God or to our fellows.

Every commitment includes a promise, whether this is expressed or not. When a man undertakes to be a Christian — whether through conversion or through the deliberate acceptance of the religion of his parents and environment — he thereby promises God to accept all the known and unknown consequences of this decision. When by my own free choice I accept myself, I promise myself to harmonize my actions, behavior and undertakings as perfectly as I can with the basic requirements of my vocation. When I choose a friend, a leader or a workmate (the choice of the two latter is generally automatically included in the choice of an association or a career) I promise to behave in accordance with this commitment. The loyalty of the soldier to his native land, of the politician to his party, of the doctor or craftsman to his professional duties, is a true commitment only in so far as these realities represent or symbolize actual persons: there is no more real commitment to abstract ideas than there is to things.

An important question arises here: is it ontologically and psychologically possible for a man to commit himself for any period of time which transcends the present moment? Does not the constant evolutionary process which characterizes the human condition make every true commitment illusory from the start? The adherents of the "philosophy of the present-moment," which is in fact supported more by literary men than by philosophers or psychologists, actually deny the claims and even the possibility of commitment. They say that man is without stability or durability, that he is the subject of a "pure" and purposeless evolution, on the physical as well as on the psychic and moral plane. According to them man is nothing more than his situation at any given moment. It would be enough for one of the elements of this situation to change or disappear, and immediately there would be another man to deal with, a man who would be totally different from the one whose place he had taken. Therefore one would not be justified in assuming that there is any psychic or moral connection between the two. The Joseph who now declares his love for Josephine will tomorrow be no longer here. The sight of another girl suffices to disturb the emotional state in which he declared his love, and that Joseph no longer exists.

Therefore, from this point of view one should only be able to commit oneself for the duration of a transitory emotional state. Indeed, no one has the right to commit another person; one may only commit one's present-self. How can I bind the man who will take my place tomorrow, or even one minute hence? I do not know this newcomer: it is impossible for me to know or guess what his spiritual qualities or external condition will be. Consequently, none of my actions or words can really commit me.

It is certain that the adherents of the "philosophy of the present-moment" also recognize that a man's social life is only possible if he becomes involved with others. Therefore they teach that one must always act as if one were really pledging oneself, as if one would be the same tomorrow as today, although we know that this is far from true. The logical conclusion of this "philosophy" is therefore that all human relationships are lies and illusions.

However shocking this attitude may seem, thus starkly expressed, it is nevertheless implicitly practiced by a significant proportion of modern, civilized human beings, probably even by many people who would object to the formulation of this thesis. Not so many years ago a famous Head of State declared that he no longer intended to respect agreements signed with other states — because he had changed his mind! Most politicians do not dare to express themselves openly with such cynicism, although many believe that political and diplomatic pacts have no truly binding force and that they may be repudiated as soon as a leader feels powerful enough to do so. These examples from the highest sphere have naturally had their repercussions in everyday life. Many people now seem to believe that treaties and solemn promises do not constitute true commitments. In private life, to mention the most obvious example, divorce has become more and more common. Even those who personally reject divorce on the grounds of their principles or the traditions of their particular environment are no longer shocked when others break so solemn and mutual a pledge as is contained in the sacrament of marriage.

"Living for the moment," as a philosophy, exercises a growing influence even over people who are unaware that it is a philosophy. It is probably the most generally practiced creed of our epoch. Therefore it is not surprising that the bonds between man and his fellow man become more and more fragile. If no new spiritual orientation comes soon the life of our society will be threatened by grave dangers. No one will be able to trust or rely upon anyone else. Between the nations there is already no real peace but only an armistice: every state is over-armed and trying feverishly to procure the most perfect instruments for war, and naturally all countries fear to be overtaken by their competitors. A similar mistrust is apparent also in government, in business, and wherever men have dealings with one another. Increased controls and supervision in every walk of life are the logical consequences of this state of mind. Even in families there is often no longer any real mutual trust.

But it is not only human relationships but the life of the individual itself that is in jeopardy because of this fear of becoming committed. A man who does not dare to commit himself whole-heartedly forfeits all possibility of true living, and becomes incapable of making a decisive choice.

A true existential commitment is only possible if man does not become totally identified with his immediate situation. Certainly, as we have already said, in a certain sense he *is* his own situation because this is inseparable from his own self. Nevertheless he transcends all his situations and proves himself their master in spite of all. Because he possesses the power to choose his own vocation and the means of fulfilling it, man is undoubtedly also capable of commitment, and indeed he commits the self which transcends his immediate situation. In spite of all his changes of circumstance his transcendent self remains the same because it contains the ontological principle of permanence.

The ontological capacity for commitment is a natural gift, but man still has to acquire the moral and psychological qualities which render this commitment possible. He has to start by recognizing the difference between his person and his situation, and so to become aware of his own identity in the midst of all the changes he himself must undergo. Whatever our theories may be, until we have experienced the reality of our own personal identity it will be hard, if not impossible, for us to commit ourselves definitely. It is not enough to know that we are capable of commitment; we must also recognize and admit that, if we wish to become real persons, commitment is a stern duty. The freedom which refuses to become involved is no true freedom. In Sartre's novel *The Ways of Freedom* Mathieu believes, according to the philosophy he has imbibed from books, that freedom is his very being, the most precious possession of all. For fear of losing this precious freedom he refuses to tie himself in marriage, or by joining a party, or in any other way. But he has to admit that this kind of freedom which allows of no commitment has no real meaning. His relations with the woman he loves and with his professor and his attitude to the war and to everyone he meets are in spite of appearances not free but closely restricted by his determination not to commit himself. This uncommitted freedom to which he is doomed becomes superfluous and useless and proves itself to be devoid of content.

Every commitment is necessarily more or less unconditional. It is absolutely, almost absolutely, or relatively unconditional according to whether it depends upon an absolute, almost absolute or merely relative choice. The man who freely and consciously commits himself to God cannot in any circumstances be released from this pledge. In the Christian religion such a commitment generally takes the form of sacraments which confer this mysterious sign, which theologians call *character*, confirmation and ordination. Those who have received one or more of these sacraments have absolutely and unconditionally committed themselves to Christ.

Whatever may occur later, nothing, not even the danger of death, can free them from this pledge: one is a Christian, or a priest, for eternity. The commitment which gives a certain direction to your life and which therefore concerns not so much your final goal itself as the means of reaching it, may be regarded as less absolute and solemn than commitment to God. Nevertheless, in practice, it must be considered as almost irrevocable and unconditional: only the higher authorities of church or state can release one from it. Marriage, religious vows, the soldier's or judge's oath belong to this category of commitments. In the two first mentioned cases, marriage and religious vows, a man pledges himself before God in a religious ceremony; in the two last mentioned cases he pledges himself to his native land which symbolizes the community of all his fellow countrymen. While the Church has never claimed the right to release a man from his status as Christian or priest, the marriage bonds are dissolved by death, and in certain cases (cf. the "Pauline privilege") even a valid marriage may be dissolved by the Church. The Church also has the right, for grave reasons, to release men and women from religious vows, and the supreme authority of the state has the right to release them from commitments to the national community.

If one has pledged oneself to an individual or a group of private individuals, the obligations which result from this pledge are only relatively unconditional. If we promise to do someone a particular service tomorrow or during the coming year we tacitly agree not to be influenced by any change in our circumstances which may occur in the meantime. Even if later on we no longer wish to honor this pledge, or if we meet another person, worthier of our service, we are nevertheless still bound by it. However irksome such an obligation may be in certain circumstances, human coexistence would be impossible without respect for the given word. Such an obligation may, however, be regarded as less binding than those we considered first: the commitment is only relatively unconditional. It will be generally admitted that the situation may change so much between the moment when the promise was made and the moment when it is to be fulfilled that we may not only be permitted, but even be obliged, to cancel the commitment.

As an example, let us take the case of a German who joined the Nazi party in 1930 because he saw in it the only means of defending his country against communism. Shortly afterwards, however, the Nazis began to persecute the Jews and the Church, to attack other countries, and to lead Germany to the greatest catastrophe of her history. What validity could still be attached to his commitment to this party? It seems to us quite clear that a German who held firm to his party pledge would be acting directly against another commitment of more profound significance: the duty to serve his country. After 1930 the situation of the German nation had become so radically altered that loyalty to the party commitment could no longer be justified.

Since there are then certain circumstances which can release men from a non-absolute commitment, we need some criterion by which to judge of what nature the circumstantial changes must be, in order to justify the non-fulfillment of an obligation. We hope that an examination of the nature of commitment will enable us to avoid both laxity and inordinate severity.

In order that the commitment should retain its binding

character the principle should be established that the changes in a person's subjective emotions are never enough to warrant his release from a commitment. This principle is to be considered binding both for promises which are almost unconditional and for those which are only relatively unconditional. Let us consider, for example, the pledges exchanged in marriage, which are normally based on mutual love. The great majority of the vows pronounced at a wedding are indisputably prompted by sincere love and contain the promise to remain united for life, according to the laws of God and of society. But young married people cannot possibly claim that they will still feel the same towards each other in twenty-five or fifty years time. Reality might gravely belie such a claim if the marriage pledges were based on emotions alone, for then they would be merely conditional and so would not constitute any true commitment, binding "for better, for worse." If there are countries or social communities in which it is permissible to arrange a divorce when there is no longer any mutual love then one must conclude that there is no longer any marriage in these countries or communities but only so-called "free love." It makes no difference, in this connection, whether the union has taken place before the authorities of the Church or before those of the state. It is only the acknowledgment of its irrevocability which makes marriage a sacred commitment. Whether the husband, in twenty-five or fifty years time, still feels the same passion for his wife as on his wedding day, or whether she is just as pretty and healthy then as before, does not alter the permanent character of the bond: the "yes" once pronounced remains always valid. Only occurrences like death, which are independent of subjective feelings, can annul the vows. One could say that very much the same thing is true of the soldier in time of war, the doctor during an epidemic, etc.

Suppose that a man has promised to keep a rendezvous, to finish a certain task by a specified time, or to lend money to a friend, these commitments have obviously not the same grave significance as those we have already mentioned. But even in these less important cases changes in subjective emotions do not give a man the right to break his word. Nevertheless, if he no longer has the promised sum at his disposal, or if he has meanwhile discovered that the man to whom he had promised to lend it is untrustworthy (had he known this before he would certainly not have promised the loan), or if his state of health is so altered that he can no longer finish his task for the specified date without harming himself, or if he is obliged to do something more important at the time of the promised rendezvous — then everyone will admit that such changed circumstances, independent as they are of the subjective emotions of the man who had given these promises, are sufficient to release him.

We must not, however, underestimate the noble example set by the "man of honor" of former times, who never withdrew a pledge once given. Every promise, however insignificant it may be, must be taken seriously. In actual fact the "man of honor" was mistaken in not differentiating in practice between truly unconditional commitments and those which are only relatively conditional, but the nature of commitment demands that one should not withdraw a reason proportionate to its importance.

One could further distinguish between the various commitments by appealing to another principle, that is, according to whether they involve only certain personal actions or whether they involve the whole person. The commitment which concerns only a few actions is only relatively unconditional: illness releases one from the promise of a visit, the loss of wealth from the promise to lend money to a friend, and so on.

The priesthood, religious vows, marriage and certain professions which directly affect the common welfare, in short, everything which is directly concerned with a man's essential vocation, involves not only certain actions but the individual himself, ontologically and psychologically. The young Christian who asks to be ordained does not merely promise to say Mass or to perform some ecclesiastical duties. If ordination demanded only this, the commitment would automatically lapse as soon as external circumstances, such as revolution or illness, prevented the priest from saying Mass or doing his duty. But in reality a man pledges his whole self in the sacrament of ordination, which raises him to a new state and is binding as long as he lives.

If in the sacrament of marriage only the reproductive capacity of the married couple were involved, then in many cases the marriage could and should be dissolved. As we have already said, the thesis in favor of divorce stems from a philosophy which denies the ontological permanence of the individual person. If the individual is an ontological reality, as we believe we have already demonstrated, then the marriage commitment involves the whole nature of man and not merely one or other of his actions or capacities. As St. Paul said, very forcibly, husband and wife become "one soul and one body." Consequently, marriage is an unconditional commitment which binds the partners for life.

Any unconditional commitment would be pointless if one had only to reckon with the static self, but in fact we commit our developing self, as far as this depends on us, that is, we commit our dynamic and potentially creative self. We are involving our future, even more than our present, selves. If the future were something already complete, which had only to be discovered and accepted, then no ontological commitment could be justified. But we know that we ourselves have to create our future, and that it will be to a great extent what we wish to make of it. In committing himself to the priesthood or to marriage, a man accepts this duty of shaping his future according to the requirements of his commitment. Husband and wife pledge themselves to ensure, by all the means at their disposal, that their union shall be capable of begetting and rearing children and of increasing their mutual love. The doctor promises not only to care for sick people but also to obtain all the knowledge he needs and continually to keep abreast of new therapeutic methods.

Until a man has entered into a commitment which irrevocably involves his whole being, past, present and future, he inevitably lives an unreal existence, merely passive or with his energies dissipated in many directions. Our lives have meaning, value and efficacy only to the extent to which they become purposeful. The chief result of true commitment is that it renders us capable of actively assuming control over the fulfillment of our mission on earth. We are indebted to it because it makes us concentrate all our energies and so become capable of playing our part in the creative effort of all mankind.

An important question therefore now arises: every commitment creates a certain bond between ourselves and those to whom we are pledged. The more important the commitment the stronger will be the bond between us. If there were only one true commitment, and that were to God alone, we should run no risk of becoming disappointed or deceived. But every one of our commitments, even those which are directly related to God, binds us to other men, in the work which we must do and the world which we will, and must, try to improve. In such circumstances what part must be played by the familiar Christian virtue of abnegation? Is there not an irreconcilable contradiction between renunciation and commitment? Particularly during the last century there were numerous prominent representatives of Christian spirituality who considered it a mistake to become involved in worldly and temporal affairs.

In a book which I have dedicated to Teilhard de Chardin I made a careful study of this question. Here I will only say that, in Teilhard's opinion and my own, the man who is brave enough to commit himself becomes at the same time, and by that very act, capable of great self-denial. However inspiring a great ideal may be, its service always means a painful struggle, abnegation, resignation and the constant sacrifice of everything that cannot be reconciled with this commitment. Because it demands from us a constant effort in a certain direction, it precludes any feeling of complacency about what we have already achieved. It is impossible truly to commit ourselves without being prepared to give up our peace and comfort. The dynamic and creative character of existential commitment will oblige us to go on perfecting ourselves until the end of our earthly life, to become, as it were, disengaged from ourselves and to be prepared to renounce even what we have already painfully won. Indeed, it is in commitment that we express the wonderful union of profound devotion and genuine renunciation.

Although it is impossible to be released from the ontological commitment which involves man's true self, yet there still remains the possibility of denying this commitment. The priest may become an apostate, the husband an adulterer. But since it is the transcendental self which is bound by this ontological commitment, no new alteration in the individual or in his external circumstances may justify such a denial. The apostate, the adulterer or the deserter cannot be released from the duties arising from their commitments, but they find themselves in a situation in which the commitment which would normally be the chief dynamic motive to drive them onwards and upwards has become a source of imminent danger.

In such circumstances are the perils which arise from unconditional commitment too dangerous to be braved? Indeed, since a mistaken notion about himself or about the person with whom he has become involved suffices to set a man irrevocably on a path which he may soon discover to be mistaken, and which he would not have followed if he had "known better," should one not logically feel bound to avoid involving oneself ontologically and irrevocably?

Because we cannot exactly foresee the future it would be dangerous to be tied to a basic situation by such a commitment, which could become a grave hindrance to one's personal development. Because of these considerations, indeed, many modern law-givers and moralists have shown themselves opposed to indissoluble marriage and to religious vows. Nevertheless, however great the dangers of commitment may be, we must hold fast to the indisputable fact that human life can become an experience of truth only through an irrevocable commitment: here, as in so many other cases, the acceptance of the challenge of life is found to be the indispensable condition for a life worthy of man. On the other hand we must also remember what we insisted upon in our first chapter: the readiness to accept a challenge is not the same thing as foolhardiness. Consequently we must never enter into a commitment lightly. Above all, it is absolutely necessary to reach an adequate psychological maturity before making such a decision. Unhappiness does not arise from doing the duties demanded by irrevocable commitments but from the fact that too frequently we have assumed these commitments without due thought. Neither religious vows nor marriages are things to be trifled with.

CHAPTER IX

THE FAITHFUL SERVANT

It is not easy to pass from the theme of commitment to that of loyalty without becoming repetitious. This is because commitment and loyalty are two closely inter-related human attitudes. As soon as man commits himself to God, to another person, a group or an ideology, he simultaneously pledges his loyalty. He begs others to have confidence in his ability and will to remain the same man tomorrow, next year and until his death. Without the vow of loyalty, which may often remain unspoken, no commitment would be of any value. If I accept another person's pledge because I believe that I can trust him, this means that I consider him to be loyal. The most surprising thing is that God himself, although he knows the weakness and instability of his creatures, accepts the commitments to him assumed by them in baptism, confirmation and ordination, and expressed in vows and every sort of solemn or private promise. The fact that God can and will trust his creatures is indeed wonderful and should make us feel proud of being men.

The numerous objections, however, which are raised against the notion of an absolute and lasting commitment now reappear in new and greater strength against the concept of loyalty, often disturbing even those who do not doubt the possibility or obligation of a commitment. If we were in eternity, they say, which means in a timeless sphere, nothing would be more normal than a pledge of loyalty. But we are in time, where everything is evolving and constantly changing. Under such circumstances a lasting loyalty is impossible for us. It is absurd and foolhardy to vow allegiance to oneself or to anyone else, for in so doing we are necessarily influenced by our present mood and by whatever the other person is like at that moment — but nobody can predict how long his present mood will last. Still less can one foresee whether the other person will deserve our loyalty tomorrow.

Very many of our contemporaries believe that a solemn vow is an inexcusable act of treachery to oneself. Naturally they do not mean treachery against a permanent self, for from the point of view of these modernists it is hardly possible to speak of a permanent self — but treachery against the evolutionary self. A man is merely his momentary situation, and this situation is not of his choosing: how then can he foresee his future? But a solemn promise implies that a man knows that he will act tomorrow towards the same person in the same way as he acts today. Any solemn pledge therefore is mere foolhardiness.

As he does not consider himself capable of pledging loyalty to another person a man will be acting illogically and rashly if he believes that he can trust another. At best, if he is a believer, he can believe and hope that God will keep the promises he made to mankind, because we know that God is the only truly unchangeable being. But the Old Testament bears witness to the fact that God keeps faith with them only in so far as they keep faith with him.

Since, however, it is impossible for us, because of our human nature, to remain faithful to God, we must not count on even God keeping faith with us. So it would seem that there is no place for loyalty in human life. Those who, in ignorance of their true condition, still try, in spite of all, to live according to the dictates of loyalty, merely expose themselves to disillusionment, painful scruples and great and useless anxiety. Consequently, loyalty not only presents an unattainable ideal but is even harmful as being a cause of psychic alienation, and it is man's duty to free himself from it as from anything else that is false and artificial.

Matrimonial loyalty is generally regarded as the proto-type of all human loyalty. According to the famous French socialist politician Léon Blum, who set himself up also as a moralist, physical loyalty between husband and wife is merely the result of social compulsion. In earlier times this compulsion was expressed in laws which severely punished adultery, but now it works through prejudices and the fear of the finger of scorn which the hypocritical society of today points at the faithless spouse. The results of such compulsion can only be disastrous, for the individual and for the happiness of the married couple. Numerous psychologists of the School of Freud are more or less of this opinion. They have filled innumerable pages with their reflections on the fundamental harm caused by the neglect of such vital instincts as the instinct for polygamy, common to male and female alike.

All theoretical or practicing believers in these theories acknowledge, however, that certain commitments are indispensable for social life, although they believe that we must not count on the loyalty of others when we wish them to remain true to us. We must simply strengthen every commitment with a great number of important safeguards, so that it will become practically impossible to withdraw from it. If one could rely upon human loyalty it would be possible to base world peace on the mutual trust of the peoples. Since this is not so the only truly effective guarantee of peace is the fear which one nation instills into others by its boasted armaments. Nor should we rely on other men's promises: in business every contract must be guaranteed by some solid securities, currency, mortgages, etc. Because there is no objective guarantee in private relationships, one should never take quite seriously the promises made to us. Particularly as regards fidelity in marriage the wisest course would be neither to demand it nor to expect it, thus avoiding at least the risk of being deceived and disillusioned.

Just because we can no longer believe in loyalty or trust, the modern world is losing its sense of humanity. Every human relationship is in danger of being torn apart by quarrels and conflicts. Friendship and love are therefore meaningless words. A certain existentialism which cares little for reality casts doubts upon our psychological capacity for loyalty which, according to Sartre, is a "dangerous virtue." Several very popular writers think that loyalty is an impediment to open-mindedness and availability, which in their opinion are the primary conditions for spiritual enrichment and development. But we hope to have already shown, in our seventh chapter, that true readiness is not the same thing as passive expectancy.

We do not underestimate the importance of many objections to loyalty, to its psychological or ontological possibility, or even to its usefulness. But one thing must be regarded as indisputable: loyalty is one of the primary qualities of the spiritual being. It is well known that there is an instinctive loyalty even in many animals, especially in dogs and horses, and the strict monogamy observed by many wild beasts and birds may give us food for thought. Certainly we see in these, as it were, mere blueprints of genuine loyalty, just as we recognize, in animal psychology, the stirrings of the spirit. We can, however, conclude from this that loyalty is at least not unnatural. True loyalty cannot be separated from the spiritual nature of man. The spirit is the principle of unity and is not subject to the common hesitations, alterations and freaks of human nature. The more a man spiritualizes himself the more his feelings and instinctive impulses help to form his personal unity.

If a man asks a friend to trust him, he implies that he is no mere freak of nature but a spiritual being. Every experience of loyalty proves and reaffirms human spirituality. Those who call themselves materialists in the philosophical sense of the word and yet demand unswerving loyalty to themselves and their party deny in practice what they preach in theory. A natural being is only capable of instinctive loyalty. On the other hand any disloyal conduct on the part of a man is like a denial of his humanity, like admitting that he is just one "thing" among many other "things."

But loyalty is even more than a proof of the spirituality of men: it also adds its own contribution to the process of our spiritualization. In order that my friend may really trust me, it is not enough for him to know that I am a being endowed with a soul: I must also pledge myself to work for the ever more intensive spiritualization of my whole being. If loyalty were only the desperate effort to revive within me a past and by-gone condition, it would soon become quite impossible. The principle of unity within me would then, in practice, have to abandon its hold on my life, and I would certainly become incapable of honoring my pledge of loyalty.

While we are promising to be loyal to one another we are also pledging our loyalty to our own particular vocation. Because of this pledge of loyalty our deeds will not be a mere series of expressions of our craving for power, for they will be directed according to our fundamental commitment. Through loyalty to his commitment man acquires the capacity to become more aware of his powers and gifts, and to use them more effectively.

* * *

As we try to prove that being loyal is both possible and useful for men we must not also claim that it is easy. At every moment we discover — in ourselves and in the world around us — invitations and temptations to disloyalty. Not only in man's inner unity a fragile thing: even his desire for unity is wavering and uncertain. Dissipation, and the disloyalty which is one of its facets, require, hardly any effort on our part. But unification — and its resultant loyalty — will always demand great and manifold efforts. For people who have long been married the many years of shared existence will have created a sort of habitual loyalty which no longer demands a positive effort, but such habitual loyalty must have required in the past innumerable acts of will and probably a difficult exercise of marital fidelity. Even now this old couple must still look upon their mutual loyalty as a freely willed commitment. If they did not do so their habitual fidelity would no longer be human loyalty but merely an empty formality. But if the habit of loyalty is sanctified by creative freedom then this spiritual value does not lessen with the years but becomes enhanced.

The higher forms of existential loyalty cannot be satisfied with merely presenting our ego with a means of self-assertion and self-indulgence: they can raise our existence to the highest degree of intensity. We think first of all of the loyalty to Christ shown by innumerable saints, a loyalty which led them to martyrdom. We think also of the patriotic loyalty of many of our comrades during the Resistance Movement of the last world war, who preferred to endure the worst tortures rather than betray the loyalty they had vowed to their comrades and their motherland.

The heroism of the "simple" marriage pledge is certainly less obvious than that of the martyrs and other champions of a lofty ideal: but it is none the less heroic. It may even be true that strict marital loyalty, especially in the moral climate of today and the conditions in which we live, demands much more strength of character than loyalty to one's faith or to one's native land. The enforced separation of many married couples, caused by war or imprisonment, may often have produced disloyalty, but it also revealed how many quite simple people of our own era are capable of determined and heroic faithfulness. When we consider the moral codes of today we see that the simple everyday fidelity of husband and wife is hardly more easy now than it was in those particular circumstances. But, whatever the circumstances may be, loyalty gives our lives that heightened intensity which enables us to feel alive. The fact that loyalty makes it possible for us to assert, to control and to ennoble our true selves does not mean that it is a form of egoism. It is not the same as pride. The faithful person is not self-seeking but directs all his energies towards the fulfillment of his vocation. He is entirely in the service of the person or cause to which he has pledged himself. The psychoanalysis of loyal people proves that they never consciously seek the aggrandizement or exaltation of their own selves, although this might be thought to be the natural consequence of loyalty. It seems to me also worthy of note that those of my acquaintances who have been most outstanding for their loyalty are not famous statesmen or successful business men but, for the most part, quite modest and simple folk. Who does not know the wonderful, almost legendary, loyalty of an old maid servant who continues to serve her master's family in good and evil times? That kind of fidelity which is not possible without personal sacrifice and effort expects no reward, not even the praise or gratitude of the family that is served. The old servant is faithful simply because she is herself. I remember the loyalty of an old peasant whom even the gravest illness could not persuade to abandon the land he had inherited from his parents; the same is true of the artisan whom one can absolutely trust to finish his daily, humble and fatiguing task, because he considers this more or less as his vocation.

* * *

Whatever tangible forms this loyalty may take, it is almost always a difficult commitment. In a certain sense it may be said to oblige us to bind temporal mobility to the changeless-

ness of eternity. For this reason one must never pledge oneself light-heartedly. The superficial charm of a young girl
which attracts a youth's admiration is not enough to justify
the deeds and words on his part which will impose upon him
the obligation of loyalty. A short lived infatuation is not
enough to compel a man to swear to God that binding loyalty
which is the mark of an ordinand's vows. When a man has to
make an important decision which necessitates a promise of
fidelity he must not be thought over prudent if he wishes to
concentrate all his energies on weighing the pros and cons
most carefully, in order to realize the full implications of his
vow. For one must only pledge loyalty when one has attained
the subjective certainty that it is in accordance with the fundamental purpose of one's whole vocation, and that it will be
no hindrance but an effective help in pursuing this.

Every promise of fidelity is freely given, even when a
man has not first taken all the necessary precautions. He must
therefore honor the obligation which leads to a commitment
that is at least "conditionally" absolute, even when it has been
entered into without due thought. Loyalty of this kind is
certainly extremely hard and can be painful. It can even become a practically unsurmountable barrier in the way of the
normal development of our personality and our temporal vocation. Many people have failed because they have committed
themselves too thoughtlessly to marriage or to the priesthood.
The Church is right when she accepts only after years of
trial the final vows of those who wish to dedicate themselves
to her service: in our opinion this trial should be in our own
days even more testing and thorough. The same thing may
be said of the role played by an engagement before marriage;
we consider it is very necessary to take a stand against the
prevailing attitude which regards an engagement as a mere
formality or, even worse, as a practically final commitment.
But once a man has declared to a woman, or a friend, or to
God: I will be true to you until death, or for eternity, he must
hold fast by this promise, however grave the difficulties and

contrasts may be. Normally, the duration of loyalty depends on the nature of the commitment: as regards the priesthood, the pledge can only be for eternity; as regards marriage, for life.

If we have admitted that we cannot pledge our word without first taking some precautionary measures, then it is our duty to allow others too to take such measures with regard to ourselves. Indeed, we have no right to accept a promise of loyalty from anyone without first having made sure that he knows who and what we are and what he is pledging. If we require loyalty from anyone, or if anyone wishes, of his own accord, to promise loyalty to us, we must, also of our own accord, offer the indispensable guarantees required by the respect due to his person. If we do not do this then we take upon ourselves a fearsome responsibility for his commitment.

* * *

Whatever the nature of the pledge we have given, whatever our subjective feelings and objective circumstances may be at the time we gave the promise, no loyalty can long survive on the strength of its first impulse. Static loyalty to something which is dead and gone cannot endure. But existential loyalty strains with all its might towards creation, towards the future, and must therefore free itself as much as possible from all that is dead and withered. The man who has pledged himself to God must certainly not be content with his own good will and the absolute purity of his intention. If he were to be satisfied with these, everything in his own nature and in the world around him which is hostile to such loyalty, would begin to undermine the integrity of his purpose. True fidelity to God requires man to play an active part in the divine plan of creation.

In the first place, we must continually strive to become more and more like God himself. We must make God's cause our own and dedicate ourselves to his service. If we do we become, to a certain extent, co-creators with God. Through this active and intimate cooperation with God our loyalty to him will become stronger, more spontaneous and more aware of itself. Then we shall no longer feel it as a burden because the creative impulse which comes from God immeasurably increases the strength of his faithful servant.

Loyalty in marriage also can only be genuine when husband and wife work creatively together. All their interchange of spiritual, emotional and physical activity must combine to build the unity of married life. This unity must, however, on no account be understood as a fixed goal: it must be expressed creatively. In the first place, it has to make its own contribution to the spiritualization of married life, to its enrichment and development. From the start no limit is set to this endeavor: we must never stop trying if we wish to avoid running the risk of subjecting marriage to a spiritual suffocation. The special nature of loyalty in marriage demands that husband and wife shall not be content merely with their own unity: they must together play their part in the creative work of God.

A true family has no right to seek only its own perfection and be content with its own immanent development. It must feel actively united with all other families as well as with the whole human community. But even this is not the most important task of the married couple: God requires them to play an active part in the creation of new human beings, who in their turn are called to seek perfection as individuals. Experience shows that the married couples who generously respond to God's wish and have many children break their marriage vows more rarely than those who decide egotistically to remain without offspring. It is in fact well known that the reason for many marriage failures lies in this refusal to share in the divine work of creation.

In the same way, the most genuine loyalty among friends stems from a common task or a common struggle for the same ideal. If this partnership in creative work is broken for any reason, even an apparently firm friendship will hardly endure for long. We may still say "my dear friend," but the spiritual bond now belongs to a dead past, and there is no longer any true friendship between us.

Remembering these examples, to which we could add many others, we believe we may assert that loyalty in all its forms loses its hold over the soul as soon as it ceases to be creative and becomes a mere formality. By force of habit, or because of some social obligation from which he does not dare to break loose, a man will still feel bound, but such a loyalty can no longer offer any true joy or enrichment to his life. A static and passive fidelity produces priests who are mere functionaries of the Church, married couples who live side by side but no longer with each other, and old friends and comrades who have nothing more to say to each other. None of these false forms of loyalty can add anything to a life which must inevitably become imprisoned in the humdrum daily round. Such loyalty is only external: a man may continue to act as a priest, a husband or a friend, but his heart is no longer there.

Perhaps we should here point out the main difference between the apostate and the convert.

The apostate or renegade has broken the vows of loyalty which had bound him to values which he served and to people with whom he lived or fought. He feels a certain resentment, a certain mysterious revulsion against them, as if he were frightened of his own conscience and feared to be drawn back into the past. The new engagements he enters into rarely seem to him revelations of new values, but more generally merely a means of justifying his infidelity to the values he has betrayed. He can talk about his past and his former friends only in a mocking or contemptuous way.

On the other hand a conversion implies the discovery and revelation of new and more sublime values. The convert does not deny his own past, nor does he feel any resentment towards it. He sees in it the providential preparation for his conversion. All the true values he has ever discovered he will preserve and try to integrate in his new existential synthesis.

He is quite convinced that conversion does not require of him any break with former loyalties, but rather confirms these: his former loyalties will be raised to the plane of a new and higher loyalty. If his former friends desert him, this will certainly cause him pain, but he will bear them no grudge.

* * *

Loyalty is based chiefly upon the innate qualities and motives of the man who pledges himself, but also on the qualities and motives of the person to whom the pledge is given: every true loyalty contains a mutual relationship. True and binding constancy can only exist in relation to people, for only people can accept our promises. Loyalty in marriage and friendship are the most useful and typical examples. As regards loyalty to a party, a class or a country, this can only be considered genuine if the party, class or country is a symbol deputizing for the living people whom it represents. But if these symbols are treated as self-sufficient absolutes in themselves, without regard for the people whom they represent, they do not deserve true loyalty for then they are nothing more than very circumscribed realities which have no right to claim a transcendental relationship with a person.

We certainly have the right to leave one class, party or group for another; in fact, we may even choose a new country without being guilty of treachery. It is just the same with ideas and with universal concepts. Our loyalty to these must always be conditional. We know from our own and others' experience that our ideas will naturally develop and change, and it is indeed our duty to allow them to develop. If we were, in the name of ideological loyalty, to deny ourselves this growth and change, our search for a true existence would be thwarted. Stubbornness in itself is merely a caricature of real constancy. We certainly do not agree with Aristotle's famous saying: "Plato is my friend, but truth is an even dearer friend"

— or at least we do not agree with it in its literal sense. Plato is a living person, and what I believe to be the truth has in general — apart from religious dogmas for believers — only a more or less temporary significance. Therefore I will not abandon my friend even if his ideas are diametrically opposed to mine.

The Christian religion, if it were merely a collection of ideas, a universal metaphysical concept or a society of believers, would have no right to claim my unconditional loyalty. If a man were to break away from it one would be justified in speaking of his spiritual development, just as one speaks of a man changing his mind if he leaves one party or philosophical school for another. In reality, however, religion does not bind us to an ideology — even the noblest — but to a real person, the divine Person. Christian doctrines and religious communities may only claim objective primacy over other doctrines and religious communities because, and in as much as, they are derived from the divine-human Person of Christ and lead us back to him. One may, and indeed must, say that there can be absolute loyalty only to God. Only in his promises can we place absolute trust; only of him can we say with absolute confidence that he will never fail us. That is why we use the word "apostasy" only for disloyalty to God.

CHAPTER X

SIN AND THE CHALLENGE OF LIFE

The psychologist should really not talk about sin, for sin is not a psychological but a theological concept. But here it is not our job to discuss the nature of sin or even to inquire whether it exists or not. The student of depth psychology is much more humble in his approach: he merely asserts that the great majority of the people known to him behave as if they were sinful, and that the majority of this majority really believe themselves to be sinners. And this is true not only of people who live in a certain civilization or in a certain period, but of people of all ages and all civilizations.

If one takes the trouble to study people more closely it is impossible to overlook the fact that there is a contrast between what they should be, in accordance with their vocation, and what they really are. Is it not astonishing that people who are called to so sublime an end feel such reluctance and so strong an aversion with regard to it? Our surprise is all the more justified when we remember that all natural creatures devote all their energies to attaining their natural end. Is it not a paradox that the only creature in the universe with a precise knowledge of his vocation, the only one who is called to fulfill it consciously and deliberately, feels impelled to reject it and in fact often cuts himself off from it? How can we understand that freedom itself, which should logically lead man to love God above all else and to yearn for what is good, is often the very cause of his downfall?

The rationalistic philosophy and naturalistic literature of the nineteenth century, which both emerged from the French "enlightenment" of the eighteenth century, asserted the fundamental goodness of human nature, although even they could not ignore the fact that there were evil and corrupt tendencies in man: egoism, greed, hatred and so on. Following Rousseau's example, however, they ascribed the evil and imperfections to defective social organization and the deficiencies of the educational system. It was therefore logical that the most generous minded people of this time tried very hard to discover better methods of education and social reform, in order to free their fellow men from the evils which burdened their lives. Utopian socialists like Fourrier, Saint-Simon and Owen, "scientific" socialists like Marx, Engels and Lenin, "positivists" like Auguste Comte and Charles Maurras, all had the same confidence in the basic goodness of human nature. If this belief — for it really was held like a faith — were true, one could consider it quite normal for a group of people who have become aware of what "true" humanity ought to be, to set up the dictatorship of the proletariat or the "government of the best minds" in order to reeducate mankind. If this belief were true it would not be impossible for a new race of men to emerge, sooner or later, men who would be innocent of egoism, sloth or any inclination towards evil.

Unfortunately, real men, as revealed to us in our own internal and external experiences, do not live up to this optimistic illusion. Not so long ago the people who did not fully share this naturalistic optimism were regarded as backward-looking "enemies of enlightenment." But today a growing number of natural scientists and philosophers feel compelled, quite apart from any religious considerations, to seek the roots of the evil which weighs so heavily upon mankind in more profound and mysterious spheres than the sphere of social order, which seems to them to be not the cause but only the symptom of the basic evil.

* * *

Readers of my books know that I too profess a certain optimism, but my optimism is grounded on something other than "pure nature." How can we fail to see that rationalism and "positivist" optimism have not fulfilled their promises? Is it not clear that the ever increasing power which man wields over the forces and energies of nature does not automatically add to his happiness, and certainly makes him no better? It is not at all improbable that man today, in spite of his better living conditions, may be less happy than the men of former times. In any case, we have seen in the most recent wars and revolutions that modern man, in spite of his higher degree of culture or civilization, is no less cruel than his primitive ancestor. However welcome many modern educational and social reforms may be it is difficult to prove that our social life today is any more enjoyable than it used to be.

For example, in the Soviet Union tremendous sacrifices and efforts have been demanded of its peoples during the last fifty years in the hope of thus forming a totally new type of man. We must, however, frankly admit that man in the Soviet Union is still far from representing the highest type of spiritual being. And this is not because the leaders of communism have been untrue to their ideas, but because the assumptions of naturalistic optimism were fundamentally mistaken.

The other kind of optimism which, for example, Teilhard de Chardin and his followers professed, has its roots not in nature but in the spirit, and for that very reason the failure of the other kind proves nothing against this optimism.

For several decades now students of depth psychology and pedagogy have become increasingly aware that the rationalist's notion of man does not fit in with any conceived or conceivable ideal but is merely a philosophical postulate. When they came to observe real individual people they had to admit that mankind is ailing in its innermost being. Kretschmer, for example, as the result of his strictly experimental study, has reached the conclusion that we are born into the world with some psychic flaw. Before our upbringing or milieu can have any influence over us we seem already more attracted to evil than to good. Superficial Freudians may have talked too much and too foolishly about children's sins, but depth psychology too has proved without a doubt that a young child is no little angel to be venerated. The French philosopher Alain also observed that there are passions in a child's soul which can become more and more harmful when ignored. But, as a materialist, he saw in these only a natural weakness which could be corrected by suitable training. The famous German pedagogue Foerster is more clear-sighted, seeing in the perverse passions of the child the expression of a real moral evil. With the awakening of consciousness we become capable of free and deliberate actions. It is, however, clear that our will is not consistent from the start, and that there is in us a struggle between good and evil inclinations. The merely external training of the child produces very meager results: at the first serious temptation the child spurns social compulsions and follows his own natural selfish impulses. In order to make education highly effective, to allow the good inclinations to overcome the evil, the will itself must be healed. Foerster therefore sees that the principal task of the teacher is to reveal to the child a more sublime love, so that he may become capable of willingly denying himself useful advantages for the sake of higher spiritual values.

What is, and whence comes, this taint or flaw which causes man to be deflected from what is good for himself and for his race and makes him long for what is harmful? Psychological experience alone is of course incapable of answering this question. Psychological analysis reveals the taint and the flaw, but cannot tell us anything about their nature and origin. Freud tried to explain our apparently innate inclination towards evil by referring to the "Oedipus complex"; this, however, is no scientific explanation but merely the interpretation of a myth to suit his own purposes.

The most eminent philosophers and psychologists who have studied the actual conditions of human life reject the rationalistic concept and boldly state that life is a drama, an endless conflict. There is certainly a certain development or progress but this does not come about gradually and harmoniously but through crises and struggles. Augustine, Pascal and Kierkegaard, who all assigned to sin a particularly important place in their concepts of man and the world, are considered even by unbelieving thinkers to be very shrewd judges of the human soul. In their opinion the tyranny of passion which defies the spirit, the innate reluctance to do good, and the ignorance and weaknesses of human nature are phenomena which spring from a mysterious source.

Even so radical a thinker as Heidegger speaks of the human condition almost in the same way as Augustine. As man is a being in time, he has tendencies and inclinations which exceed his awareness. When we say that he is a being in time we mean that he is now a fallen being, degraded to a level of life which gives him no cause for pride. Space and time are not merely the conditions of our existence; they form a prison from which the spirit seeks in vain to escape. If man were not a fallen being it would be impossible to cope with his situation. His fear and grief are the proofs of his fallen state (see *Sein und Zeit*).

Heidegger is not the only modern thinker who believes that man is a fallen creature. Many others too are convinced that the present condition of mankind is not normal: it seems so absurd and tragic. According to them, suffering and death and the unavoidable conflict between the spirit and freedom are not to be accepted as the natural condition of spiritual beings. With the advancement of knowledge offered us by depth psychology it is becoming more and more obvious that man as understood by rationalistic and positivist philosophers, exists nowhere but in their imagination. Real man is a fallen creature, or at least is sick. It is impossible to understand the condition of man, and even more impossible to prescribe a rule of life for him, unless we take into consideration the corruption of the human race and the lack of harmony between his present state and the most profound needs of his conscious being. How can one speak of love or of the family, the organization of society, work, property, war and peace, without taking into account this corruption and its consequences?

The Marxists are today almost alone in believing in the natural goodness of man and in attributing all the evil in the world to a faulty economic situation. Naturally we do not believe that man is incapable of true goodness, or capable only of evil. But it is clear that in the world around us what is good can only be attained in the midst of individual and collective evil. Neither the progress of science nor social training is capable of controlling the disorder of our instincts, our will and our reason. Almost everything that Freud wrote about the *libido* and its destructive power was already well known to Augustine, but he called it concupiscence. This concupiscence, the consequence of original sin, is according to Augustine the root of all our sins, just as Freud's *libido* is said to be the cause of all human perversity. The worst mistake that teachers and psychologists can make is therefore to treat man as if he were spiritually sound. Because man is psychologically infirm he is seen to be a living contradiction, his life is full of conflict, and his very freedom may lead him to self-destruction. It is wrong to regard psychopathology contemptuously as the science of the abnormal, as if the abnormal were the exception, the rare occurrence. In fact it constitutes an important part of psychology and anthropology. It is not by accident that most psychological discoveries were made by means of clinical experiments. Neither philosophers nor teachers, and certainly no priests, can neglect the study of the sick mind. Adam is the symbol of the first and last "normal" man (we are not speaking of Christ, the God-Man); all his descendants are pathological cases, the difference merely consisting in the degree and nature of the abnormality.

From what we learn from experience and from Christian revelation, the concept of sin includes much more than the notion of corruption. There can indeed be no sin for us personally, or for mankind as a whole, without our sharing in some way in the responsibility for this evil. Our personal freedom is in some way implicated in this drama which has turned our lives into a tragedy. For Socrates sin was identical with ignorance and a victory over ignorance was also a victory over sin. For many modern thinkers who do not like to use the word "sin," it is a guilt consciousness that has no objective cause, or a fatality against which man can do nothing. In both these hypotheses sin is seen as a terrible injustice, and this point of view justifies the outraged cries and blasphemies against God who is held responsible for the sufferings, wars and all other miseries of humanity. And those who do not believe in any God can maintain that the whole of life is an absurdity, because apparently there is no way of escape from this fatal degradation.

Only the Christian point of view allows us to understand sin neither as a fatality nor as an absurdity but as the free action of a spiritual being, in which both his reason and his free will are involved. Theoretically one may even talk about "natural sin," which would consist in disobedience against the natural law, but in our opinion the distinction between natural and divine law is artificial because the concept of "pure nature" is quite undefined and of only speculative value. For the believer every sin is sin against God. Kierkegaard says very rightly that the concept of sin leads us into the sphere of sacred and religious ideas, for God and sin are two correlative concepts. As soon as man sees himself as a sinner he enters into a relationship with God, even if he doubts or denies God's existence.

If sin were a purely "natural" occurrence one might hope one day to find a suitable means of doing away with it, partly or totally. This was in fact the daring hope of psychoanalysts. But sin is of a religious origin. Even if science could abolish disease, suffering, and death itself, if statesmen could establish a lasting peace among nations, classes and individuals, man would still be a sinful creature, forever incapable, by his own unaided strength, of fulfilling his vocation as co-creator with God. In order to free man from the servitude of sin God's intervention is absolutely indispensable. Teilhard de Chardin and his followers have been quite wrongly accused of denying the reality of sin, but it is because we are convinced of its religious nature that we do not speak of it in books about the natural sciences. We all accept with gratitude that completion of our natural knowledge which is given us in revelation.

Redemption, as Christian revelation has taught us, does not consist primarily and chiefly in the repairing of the damage caused by sin in the cosmic order and in men's souls. In spite of Christ's death on the Cross and his Resurrection most of the disorder caused by sin is still with us and there is little hope that scientific and social progress will ever completely conquer it. Redemption is mainly a matter of spiritual and moral healing, of the restoration of the religious relationship between God and men, and it promises the total rebirth of man and of the whole universe on the "Day of the Lord." It is characteristic of sin that it gives rise to new sins. Every moral failing obscures the reason and sets a new obstacle on our path to freedom. The greater the part that reason and freedom play in a sinful action the graver the sin. As man is often to blame for the weaknesses of his reason and of his will, he must bear the responsibility also for sins and mistakes which he neither foresaw nor willed. But on the other hand his reason and his freedom are not divine but human, which means that they are never absolute. And so we find ourselves once more in the already familiar and ambiguous situation of being sinners, and yet without sin.

In the end every sin can be defined as a lack of faith. If our faith in God were strong enough, that is, not merely a belief in the existence of God and the truth of revelation, but a faith like that described by St. Paul, steeped in love and hope, then we would freely wish to do only the will of God, and there would be no more sin.

For the atheist philosopher Sartre, who is also speaking of fundamental sin, this is, as it were, a fatality of the human condition. We, instead, think that it should be regarded rather as a challenge. Although Christian theology links all individual sins with fundamental or original sin, it asserts that human nature is not entirely corrupted by them. Our reason is still capable of recognizing natural truth: it is only our supernatural calling which will remain unattainable unless we receive special grace from God. Even our freedom is not wholly perverted. The main consequence of sin is concupiscence, which restricts the spontaneity of our good impulses and often makes us prefer the immediate interests of the individual to the higher interests of the human person. But one must never forget that since Christ has redeemed the world, everyone has the power to resist the ravages of original sin and to free himself from personal faults.

* * *

Is fundamental or original sin really a sin? Or is it not rather a sort of metaphysical corruption which the Jews and Christians took to be the consequence of the first man's sin, which he passed on to us, rather in the same way as a person suffering from alcoholism or syphilis passes on his illness or its consequences to his descendants? If we thought this was the case, we might even admit that this fundamental corruption explains our weakness and our helplessness, which are the source of our personal shortcomings and misdeeds.

But then we should bear as little responsibility for these as the son of a syphilitic man bears for his disease. In so far as personal failings are caused by original sin, they would no longer be real sins. We should be burdened with them psychologically and physically, but we should be morally innocent. The feeling of guilt experienced by Francis of Assisi, Pascal, Kierkegaard and many other deeply religious people who did not personally commit any grave sins would be an illusion, a dangerous psychic malaise. Many psychoanalysts and psychopathologists are in fact determined to find some sort of suitable clinical treatment for this "neurosis."

We freely admit that reason, which trusts only its own light, can hardly conceive how anyone can be held personally responsible for a sin committed in the uncertain past by an uncertain forefather in an uncertain way. Sartre is perhaps the only philosopher of our own times who explicitly assigns to man the total responsibility for all he is and does. But, as we have already pointed out, Sartre interprets freedom in a peculiar way, identifying it with determinism. Traditional Christian teaching, instead, claims that original sin is truly the sin of all mankind, because if this were not so we should have had no need of a Redeemer. Naturally, it is not within the competence of the psychologist to adopt an authoritative attitude to these questions. We modestly content ourselves with trying to understand from what point of view such a thesis can be asserted and what it can explain. So it seems to us significant that the majority of Christians of the last generation understood the general responsibility for original sin hardly any better than did the rationalists: they were willing to believe it merely because it was the teaching of the Church.

Rampant individualism has indeed not spared even the educated Christian. Everyone stands before his God as a small, self-contained and autonomous unit, self-sufficient and self-satisfied. He works for his own salvation, trusts in his own merits and good works, and fears chastisement for his own sins. From the point of view of this individualistic spirituality the indissoluble link between persons and generations constituted by the sins committed by their forefathers can be neither understood nor experienced, any more than we can understand acquiring merit for another person. We do not feel responsible for the sins of others. "The difficulty," wrote Voltaire, speaking as the authoritative spokesman of his age, "is to understand how our souls today, which are but newly created, can be held responsible for a sin committed so long ago." From the individualistic point of view moral responsibility presupposes the solitariness of man. The famous forerunner of psychoanalysis, Paul Janet, expresses this thesis: "How could I have done this when I was not yet born? Unless we admit the theory of the pre-existence of souls, or of a sort of humanistic pantheism, we cannot understand the theological dogma that all have sinned in Adam."

In order to be able to understand something of the mystery of original sin, and consequently of the moral solidarity of all men, we must not only sever the link with rationalism — as most present day psychologists and philosophers have already done — but we must give up any individualistic conception of man and of his relationship with God and the world. The mysteries of the Christian faith can be understood only from the Biblical point of view, which is not individualistic but fundamentally communal and universal. When we read the Bible it is obvious that God did not create Adam merely as an individual, but as the First Man. Not for his own individual salvation was Abraham chosen, but as the leader of the chosen people. Not to individuals but to the people were entrusted the law and the promises. Christ himself came, not to save individuals, even in great numbers, but to create a new "people of God, the Church, of which he is the Head."

We become Christians by joining the Christian community. Individual salvation can only come about within the shared salvation of the Mystical Body. John, Paul and the Fathers of the Church are always insisting on the communal character of the Christian faith. The Eucharistic Meal surely represents the most sublime personal communion between the soul and God, but also and at the same time the communion between brothers and between all Christians and the Church. To deny a brother Holy Communion means to exclude him from the Christian community.

This spiritual community and solidarity of all men ought not to be too difficult for educated people of our time to grasp. Already, in the realm of the natural order, the most personal things in our lives are seen to be interpersonal. We all breathe the same air and move in the same intellectual atmosphere, and all our actions intermingle. It is difficult, if not impossible, for us to say with any certainty what our own individual contribution is in all our most personal and spontaneous reactions and convictions, and what elements are contributed by our milieu, the books we have read, the people who live in our vicinity and whom perhaps we hardly know, or those who lived thousands of years before us. The most important intellectual conquest of our time is not the discovery of the atom bomb but the present almost universal realization of human solidarity in good and evil. It surprises no one any longer when novels as well as philosophical works declare the collective responsibility of a people, a class, an era or even a whole civilization or mankind in general. It is universally understood that the "sins" of my people, of my social class or my era are indeed my sins, although as an individual I did not commit them. If I want to be absolved from them, I must disassociate myself explicitly from them, and by deeds rather than by words, and brave the dangers inherent in such an attitude. Many German anti-Fascists did this, and many Frenchmen during the Algerian war.

In his novel *The Brothers Karamazov* Dostoyevsky very well presented this question of collective responsibility. Wrongly accused of having killed his father, but conscious of having committed many other despicable crimes, Mitja consents to be condemned for patricide because, as he says, "we are all responsible one for another." And Sosim counselled Aljoscha: "Take upon your own shoulders the sins of others. ... If you consider yourself truly responsible for all men and for everything they do you will soon understand that you are indeed to blame for all and everything. If I myself were a good man perhaps there would be no more criminals."

Collective guilt and responsibility can be understood only when mankind is no longer considered as a more or less numerous crowd of individuals thrown together no one knows how or why, in time and space. There is a true unity of the human race, which is not so much a present reality as a duty, which belongs rather to the future than to the past. The unity is naturally not physical but psychological and metaphysical. Whatever we may do, we can never succeed in detaching ourselves from our fellows. We can cease to belong to a nation, a class or a certain civilization, but we cannot cease to be human beings. We may approve or disapprove of mankind in general, but its reality remains, independent of our will.

From this it follows that the sins committed by us are not merely our own sins. In our refusal to live with God and to respond generously to his call, we involve all our fellow men. Our own sins are the more or less direct cause of sins in others, and vice versa. As long as we are sinners ourselves we are truly responsible for all the sins of the world. Mankind must be understood as a vast family of sinners, and all men's sins are intermingled in such a confusion that God alone can impute to each one his share of responsibility. No one may, like Pilate, wash his hands of other men's sins. Mankind as a whole has denied to God the obedience due to him. As a member of the human family I share all its greatness but also all its weaknesses and failings.

Every sin stains our soul and more or less restricts our freedom, but, however serious the challenge of sin, we are not necessarily condemned because of it to a purposeless existence. Sin can even play a very positive role in our lives by making us more aware of our freedom. The sinner well knows that before he sinned he was free, to sin or not to sin, and also that he is free even after sinning, free to assume this or that attitude to the sins he has committed.

CHAPTER XI

FEAR, UNREST AND ANXIETY

Again we find ourselves in agreement with Kierkegaard, and also with Augustine and Pascal, for these three profound Christian thinkers saw in anxiety, in existential disquiet, the dialectical force which jerks the free but imperfect man out of his banal existence and plunges him into a life full of challenge. But on no account must existential disquiet or anxiety be confused with neurotic fear, which achieves no positive results.

Anxiety arises from the contradictions of human nature, of which we have already spoken, and from the fact that we are never quite what we are intended to be, because we are in a state of constant evolution. According to Kierkegaard, we are not merely restless, we are also full of fear, because we are sinners. Fear and sin are, in his opinion, two correlative concepts. Fear means desiring what we are afraid of, and this is particularly true of sin. Through the enjoyment and heightened experience of individual freedom, both of which are promised by sin, it exercises a powerful attraction over us all, but at the same time it alarms us too, because of the disorder it creates and the opposition and hostility which it introduces into our relation with God. Being torn this way and that between love and hatred of sin, we suffer from an anxiety which in certain circumstances may turn into neurotic fear.

The state of anxiety is closely linked with our notion of what is possible. A deed or an occurrence, which we consider impossible may give rise to feelings of longing or regret but, however great the love or horror it inspires, cannot produce the state we call anxiety. If we happen to feel troubled because of a past occurrence or deed, our anxiety does not stem from the past itself but from our fear of its present consequences. According to Kierkegaard's concept of sin, anxiety is caused either by the fear of the possibility of a future sin or by the feared and hoped for consequences of a past sin.

It is true not only that sin produces a sense of disquiet but that very often this disquiet itself leads to sin. Therefore it is not always true that fear is the beginning of wisdom or that fear of sin protects us from it. Sin must be understood as the transition from good to evil. If, however, we analyse psychologically the actual conduct of the sinner, we shall see that very rarely, if ever, can we pass directly from a state of innocence to a state of sin. Sin first reveals itself to our conscience as a possibility. From the moment when this possibility begins to seem in any way desirable, we are no longer in the state of innocence because that state knows neither evil nor its fascination. As long as evil remains undesirable we are still innocent. This mingling of love and hate for sin in our soul brings about a state of disquiet and unrest which turns to anxiety. It is, however, psychologically impossible to remain in this state without seeking to assuage this anxiety. If our freedom allows itself to be tempted by the attraction of sin the innocent of one moment become the sinners of the next. Even when sin has been committed this does not assuage the anxiety, although before sinning we may have thought that it would. In fact, sin leaves us with a feeling of guilt, a burdened conscience. The sinner feels guilty and guiltless at the same time, although he knows he is no longer innocent. Has he not become a victim of the circumstances in which he found himself? Was it not just his state of fear before sinning which caused him to sin? And yet he knows well that he is not innocent. He knows that he flirted with the fatal circumstances. If he preferred to feel the fascination rather than the horror of sin his freedom must surely have been involved. This ambiguous situation — guilty or guiltless? — produces new anxiety. A man would like to recapture his former innocence, for now he sees in it a beauty of which he was formerly unaware. If the desire to restore his innocence predominates, then his anxiety leads to remorse which is capable of causing conversion and a spiritual ascent. But if he is discouraged by the realization of his weakness, then his anxiety may induce him to commit a new and even graver sin. It is therefore once more in the exercise of his human freedom that he must decide which part the anxiety connected with sin should play in his life.

* * *

The case of the sinner which we have already examined will serve as a typical example of the transition from the concept of the feasibility of an action to the action itself in the dialectic of anxiety. Anxiety is not only caused by the attraction or horror felt for the sin but is aroused also in the case of every existential choice which man has to make. This anxiety arouses freedom from its state of indifference or inertia and forces it to make a decision. In this way it has its own part to play in our lives. It belongs to the dynamic structure of the soul and contributes to the fulfilling of our vocation. It is like a goad which urges us on our way and forbids us to content ourselves with a mediocre success.

Anxiety and disquiet are proper only to a creature in an ambiguous state. Man is an astounding mixture of the temporal and the eternal, the finite and the infinite, predestination and freedom. Amidst these contradictory elements of human nature there is seldom any harmony, in fact much more frequently a fierce conflict in which sometimes one side and sometimes the other is victorious. The freedom of the individual is not however entirely obliterated, and man can never be satisfied with a state of conflict in his soul. All his wishes and endeavors are directed towards the restoration of his disrupted unity.

The most habitual temptation of the man troubled by anxiety or restlessness is the temptation to try to get rid of one of these antitheses in his life. There are still many people, especially in religious circles, who are ashamed of their bodies. All their bodily desires and needs seem to them unjustified, and so they feel they must deny them any satisfaction. They are willing to recognize only the more sublime aspirations of the soul, and they wish to live like angels. But the body, with all that it stands for, cannot so simply be set aside, and it does not take long to relegate the lusts of the flesh to the realm of the subconscious. When we least expect it our body takes its revenge and wrecks the beautiful but artificial construction of a spiritualized life.

Others, instead, forget human greatness and transcendence and really believe in their claim to live only according to the established and irresistible laws of the body. They pamper and adore it, listen to its merest whisper, and satisfy all its capricious demands. They hope in this way to smother all the anxiety and disquiet in their souls and to experience only peace and pleasure. But in reality psychic unity and the repression of existential fear can no more be effected in this way than they can by "spiritual" people. To all appearances these people live wholly for their bodies and seem satisfied with their lives, but at some time or other, in good or evil fortune, in the face of death or of some decisive choice, the repressed anxiety will return to trouble their souls, perhaps in the form of a neurotic fear.

The repression of existential anxiety may de-humanize man and impoverish him spiritually, but it can never restore his psychic unity. The annihilation of anxiety would mean the annihilation of life itself. Instead of trying to banish all spiritual disquiet we should entrust to it the task of restoring our personal integrity. For man cannot achieve integrity by annihilating one of the component elements of his complex human nature but only by integrating them all in a loftier synthesis. So long as our earthly life endures this synthesis will never be perfect and a certain disquiet will always remain with us. Good and evil will always be with us, giving rise to ever new conflicts, rivalries and anxieties — but they will also be the cause of new spiritual progress.

Even saints and heroes never succeed in achieving total integration. In fact, the more a man perfects himself the more he becomes conscious of the contradictions within him. This awareness will of course increase his dissatisfaction with himself and his desire for unity. The greater his spiritual unrest the more heavily he feels burdened with sensuality, which opposes his loftiest aspirations. We must not smile, therefore, when we read that great saints like Francis of Assisi and the holy hermit Anthony were terribly distressed by the lusts of the flesh although they were already revered as saints. Their bodies must have been infinitely more subject to the spirit than ours are — but just because their psychic integrity was almost perfect they were very acutely aware of the slightest dissonance, and so they felt an anxiety which seems unreal to ordinary people. In fact, the true source of anxiety is not the body but the soul.

* * *

It would be wrong to see existential anxiety as something purely subjective, as a drama which takes place only in the individual consciousness. It is indeed true that modern existentialism has preferred to analyse and describe the individual subjective aspect of anxiety, with the result that we are induced to think that it merely makes men turn inward on themselves and so renders them unfit for any life struggle. Consequently, the man of action considers anxiety to be a symptom of neurosis, which must be treated with contempt. It is, however, a mistake to speak of a conflict between "subjective" and "objective," between "individual" and "social." Our condition as creatures, placed in this world as members of a human community, certainly does not require us to banish all individual anxiety, for this also can serve to further social progress.

Human anxiety is undoubtedly just as contradictory and ambiguous as the individual soul. Individuals set themselves against other individuals, classes against other classes, nations against nations and even continents against continents. Although we have become aware of the close material and spiritual solidarity of all men, we must admit that the peace and harmony which should rule mankind are not yet with us. Technical and cultural progress has not yet succeeded in smoothing out these contrasts. France and Germany are reconciled, to be sure, but the hostility between East and West is even more menacing than the previous inherited national enmity. In short, the world today is more deeply split asunder than ever before. How then must a man, who is eager to live his life to full, consider the drama of the world around him, which forms his own situation and in a certain sense his ego? The attempt to flee from the "wicked world" and place oneself outside the conflict, is made very frequently. Many of our contemporaries would like to escape from it all, to withdraw to distant lands and lonely islands; they are always looking for less disturbed, more tranquil corners of the world! But if they do set out they generally find themselves faced with new contradictions and conflicts; they have chosen for themselves not freedom but another servitude.

Among Christian thinkers the attempt to flee from the world often ends in the formation of small groups of the élite. Some hide in remote and deserted villages, to live there in a sort of primitive simplicity, far from the strife and misery of the world. Others remain with us but gather friends around them and try as far as possible to forget the bad and sinful world. Most of these attempts are inspired by a very real purity of intention, a desire for spiritual perfection. But the Christian is not allowed to enjoy the artistic *chaleur* of a ghetto. He will soon become aware of his treachery and cowardice, of his disloyalty to his fellows and to the work which God has entrusted to him in the world. Regrettable as it may be, there exists no island where man can with impunity escape from human bondage.

Others hope to achieve inner serenity simply by closing their eyes to reality and persuading themselves that all is for the best in the best possible world. They carry on their business, go in for politics, take it upon themselves to ensure the careers and futures of their children, and try to have the largest possible share of temporal joys and pleasures — without caring about what the morrow will bring. But in this present world of ours such behavior cannot last for long. There is no wealth which we can count on as permanent, no way of ensuring a peaceful old age. Sooner or later we become aware of the close bonds which link our individual destinies to the common destiny of our epoch and our country, and then we are back once more in this broken down old world. Whatever we may do, we remain creatures of this world and as such we cannot disassociate ourselves from the conflicts, sorrows and efforts of our fellow beings. The world flows in upon us from all sides, so that it is impossible to escape its anguish. Whether we like it or not, the greatness and the misery of our epoch or class or country are also our own greatness and our own personal misery. It is not at all surprising that we are afraid of the consequences which may arise, for ourselves and for others, from our close involvement with the world.

Life in the human community presents a new dilemma to men and is consequently a new source of anxiety. Although now a social unease, and no longer a merely personal anxiety, it weighs just as heavily upon our consciences. All the various attempts to smother it or escape from it are mere subterfuges. The right way to overcome it lies in a courageous acceptance of the actual world situation and of the real solidarity of all peoples. This is no passive acceptance. In the same way as the individual, all men together strive to restore the unity broken by sin. The climax reached today in the conflicts between classes, ideologies and peoples may be taken as a proof that men are now most actively engaged in the restoration of the unity of mankind. It is no longer a case of the worker opposing the employer, but of the proletariat opposing capitalism. It is no longer a case of one nation threatening to wage war on another but of half the world threatening the other half. But even in these immense conflicts and cleavages we may dare to perceive the signs of an increasing endeavor to establish unity, and so we remain optimists in spite of all.

Social unease will impel us to play our part in mankind's struggles for unity, for a world in which there will be more justice, brotherhood and love. It is not enough merely to be aware of the problem: knowledge must lead to action. We must have no fear of the unavoidable challenges of life and we must never attempt flight. Our disquiet will give birth to creative joy.

But here also matters are much more complicated than many people think. Driven by social anxiety, many believe that they must commit themselves unreservedly to a party or "movement." The totalitarian parties have a special predilection for such followers, who willingly submit to strict discipline and offer blind and unconditional obedience. Out of these are formed the groups of "activists" who are "ready for anything." In favorable circumstances they sometimes prove to be a fearsome and most destructive force.

The man who has chosen this way feels at first a profound

relief. He need no longer ask what he must do or say, he need look for nothing more. He feels quite safe and his life appears to have become meaningful and useful to society. All anxiety seems to have been finally banished. As the price for this feeling of security it is true that he has been obliged to renounce his freedom, but this loss seems to him quite insignificant in comparison with the usefulness and efficiency his actions now apparently possess. The thought that along with his freedom he has also renounced his human dignity never bothers him. He generally becomes so used to acting, and even to thinking, according to the orders of his party that he becomes a sort of automaton. While still giving good service to his party's cause, he is no longer capable of any personal initiative or any creative activity. The parties which demand such self-annihilation from their adherents may for a while seem very strong and effective, but as soon as the period of struggle for the conquest of power is over they are incapable of any creative work. However "dynamic" and "dialectical" their ideology was at the start it soon crystallizes into empty slogans. A society built by these robot men would not be a human community but a sort of mass agglomeration.

* * *

Although the challenges of a true life are terrifyingly great, I am nevertheless still optimistic about the future of mankind. My hope and my deepest conviction are that there will always be men who will not allow existential dissatisfaction to degenerate into neurotic fear, and so will not seek escape in a subhuman existence. If the totalitarian regimes should succeed temporarily in setting up a "mass" or "beehive" society, I hope that man's innate longing for freedom would be strong enough one day to allow existential dissatisfaction to express itself once more against such a construction. The man who, dissatisfied with the social order, has accepted his condition in time and place and refused to deny the reality of the human condition finds himself in a new dilemma: if he is satisfied with the furtherance of his own individual vocation then he will try to be a superman, a *Führer* or a *Duce*, who, for the sake of satisfying his lust for power, will not shrink at the thought of enslaving millions of other men, trampling upon their freedom and degrading them to the state of mere things. But the man who is conscious of his condition and his calling knows that such an assertion of the will to power allows the supposed superman merely a spurious freedom which can only end in destruction. The fufillment of our own lives cannot be separated from the fulfillment of all other lives. Social progress must promote the development of all individuals, and every individual, conscious of his own vocation, must seek to promote social progress.

The gradual awareness of this fundamental link between social and individual progress leads to a new anxiety. In order to contribute effectively to the building of a new order of society worthy of mankind it is not enough to cherish a noble ideal. Fine intentions must be transformed into actions. Not in the realm of the imagination, but in our real world must our activity find its scope. It can only be effective when it fits the actual circumstances of our own time and civilization. But our situation is not a simple one. Many people of our era, who have become aware of the need for a fundamental revolution in society, come up against the reality of communism. This seems indeed to them the only effective force which can claim to remold the world entirely. The communist believes he is in possession of the only theory that works, and that he is capable of the necessary audacity, discipline and energy to put it into practice. In my youth what made the greatest impression on me and on many others was the realization that communism enjoyed the confidence of the majority of the working classes and of the most thoughtful members of the so-called economically developed societies, and consequently of those social classes which have most to suffer from present injustices and so make the greatest effort to reform the world. It would therefore be logical to require that all those who wish to help mankind to reach a higher stage of development should work together with communism. After the second World War, and especially in France and Italy, this necessity seemed unavoidable to many high-minded Christians, and in many countries in South America and Africa it still seems so today.

But a closer observation and a longer experience show that our situation is considerably more complicated than had been thought at first. The methods of propaganda, power seizure and domination employed by communism have shown themselves clearly and radically opposed to human dignity. Lies and clumnies, political falsifications and systematic agitations are much more used by communism than by any of the other parties which we treat with such reserve and mistrust. Party activists are expected to renounce all personal judgment and to give blind obedience to the currently prevailing ideas of the party leadership. Yesterday Stalin was to be venerated like a god, today he must be regarded as the wickedest of barbarians. Is it not obvious to any thinking man that it is impossible with such methods and tactics to build a new and better world in which freedom, truth, human dignity, happiness and understanding may prevail? And in reality there is in Russia, as in all the other lands where communism has seized power, neither material nor spiritual freedom, neither general prosperity nor joy in living.

It follows then that no honest friends of social progress have the right to contribute in any way to the victory of communism: by so doing they would be opposing the main purpose of the changes which must come about. Is it not clear that the revolution of the present world order can only be effected on condition that human dignity, both material and spiritual, be safeguarded?

Naturally, this awareness increases our fears for society: is there no chance of directing the social life of men to a high purpose? Are the failures of the communist experiments sufficiently obvious to make all profound social reforms seem merely Utopian dreams? Must we therefore hope to promote the progress of mankind through individual conversions alone? As is well known, numerous very talented men, after being disillusioned by communism, have given up all forms of social activity. Some have become individualistic aesthetes, others have become resolute supporters of Fascist counter-revolutions. In various ways they all try to escape from this anxiety about human society.

In our opinion neither of these ways is good. We may not use the experience of disillusionment as a pretext for saying: "There can be no better order than the present, and we must be satisfied with improving it a little as opportunity arises." It is not true that the plans and projects for a brighter future are already doomed to failure. It is our firm conviction that optimism with regard both to the individual and to society is a thousand times more justifiable than pessimism. The perfection for which we yearn is not behind but before us. Human freedom, however little esteemed by men, is creative. All who wish to force it to choose between ready made solutions such as communism, Fascism, capitalism and so on, and who say that these represent our only way of escaping from this troublesome state of anxiety, ignore the true nature of freedom. It is in fact not a mere capacity to choose between several alternatives but, also and even more, a power of discovery and invention. It must therefore be possible to discover totally new forms of social communal life, which do away with the injustices of the old world and promote the welfare of all without degrading human dignity. We find ourselves agreeing with the Senegalese President Leopold Sedar Senghor who believes he has found in the teachings of Teilhard de Chardin the inspiration to vanquish both capitalism and communism, and so create what he calls "African Socialism."

The anxiety, however, which arises from the social contrasts and contradictions of the world today must not be suppressed. It must lead to the discovery and creation of something really new. This inventive and creative work will certainly be more difficult than the choice between ready-made solutions, but it will work effectively for human unity, for which all the vital forces and generous longings of our age are consciously or unconsciously striving.

* * *

Existential anxiety, therefore, does not lead, like neurotic fear, to inactivity and passivity. On the contrary, if we listen to its voice, it will prepare us for the most effective and authentic activity. Great men of action, like all true creators, suffered from existential anxiety about the individual and about human society.

Our era is probably spiritually and sociologically more restless than past centuries. But it would be a mistake to interpret this restlessness as a sign of the decadence of an overcivilized humanity. The annihilation of anxiety would not lead us to divine simplicity but much more probably to a state of animal squalor. Anxiety is the mark of human youth and vitality when it is not allowed to remain sterile and to turn to neurotic fear. Let us remain optimistic about mankind today, in spite of all the weaknesses and miseries of our era, and precisely because we perceive this profound disquiet in the depths of men's souls. For this reason we may hope that the present religious, moral, intellectual and social crisis, far from signifying a death agony, may represent the growing pains of a humanity in which the grace of Christ has been working for two thousand years, and which has reached a new and decisive turning point in its spiritual evolution.

Moreover, no man can totally avoid existential anxiety. The least sensitive men — which means the least spiritualized — as well as those who are most sensitive to the spirit, all share in the general anxiety of mankind. The pettiness and dissipations of everyday life are usually ineffective means through which we try to rid ourselves of the anxiety inherent in the human condition, because we lack the courage to allow ourselves to face this disquiet. Just as it is impossible for us to escape from the human condition, so we cannot escape from this anxiety. But we can make a good or bad use of both. The danger is that anxiety may degenerate into neurotic fear if for conscious or unconscious motives we deny the dialectical need of our existence to rise to progressively higher levels of being. But, if we accept existential anxiety as a dialectical experience, it will become the most important dynamic force in our creative development. It breaks down all restrictions, and all the barriers set up by psychological and sociological determinism, and prevents us from contenting ourselves with lazy half solutions. It spurs us forwards and upwards, and encourages us to be ready at any moment for inventions and discoveries. All that is imperfect in us, all idols and false values, will be consumed by this anxiety. It demands that we shall struggle against all that is ambiguous and perverse in ourselves and in the world around us — in order that we may restore the unity of mankind and all creation.

*   *   *

The saint who has truly realized, as perfectly as is possible in time, the unity of his own ego and his unity with God, will therefore never be free of existential anxiety. But in his case, it no longer has as its main theme or cause the personal situation of the individual in the world and his relation to God, but the unfolding of all God's work in time. How can a man who has surrendered himself to God be free of anxiety as long as there are still people who do not know God and do not love him above all else, who hate each other and whose defiance is an obstacle to the setting up of God's kingdom? This anxiety drove Francis of Assisi to wander all his life from town to town, from village to village, to induce his fellow men to make peace with each other and to become aware of their sublime vocation as children and co-workers with God. It compelled Francis Xavier and thousands of other missionaries to leave their homelands forever in order to proclaim Christ's message to the most distant peoples. The most sublime spiritual dissatisfaction, in which the individual himself hardly counts any longer, and which is mainly inspired by zeal for God's glory, is evidently very different from ordinary anxiety and fear. As we have already stated, fear of sin is ambiguous and troublesome because both love and fear are present in it at the same time. It may lead to repentance but it may also lead to despair. The disquiet which stirs the saint's soul knows no such ambiguity; it loses itself in the deepest peace of the soul, and in its happiness. With its aid we can only go forwards and upwards.

CHAPTER XII

PASSION AND ITS CHALLENGE

Only if our life is borne forward on the wings of a great passion can it become great and beautiful. I know that this assertion may sound shocking to many because, according to the all too widely diffused rationalistic preconceptions, all decisions and actions must be based on coolly objective reasoning alone. In order that rational objectivity may not be disturbed, the rationalists demand the exclusion of all emotional factors, especially of passion which is the strongest of all. Not only our choice of an occupation or calling, but also our choice of a marriage partner must be rational. Even before we give alms we must make sure that the beggar is a worthy recipient. Numerous Christians have blinded themselves out of that respect for reason which was so widely diffused in the nineteenth century, and so they have allowed the division between the rational and the affective to appear even in their moral and religious life. The Christian life, they asserted, must be entirely founded on reason: morals and dogmas alike must satisfy its requirements. As it seemed impossible to make mysticism also reasonable, it was generally suspected and rejected. The passions and affections, whose presence in our most profound being cannot be denied, were seen as the result and symbol of evil and sin. Even the shameful sins of which no one could speak in decent society were inspired by passion, as were crime and adultery, but not an honest and worthy life.

The bad reputation of affectivity, and particularly of passion, has certainly been largely responsible for the fact that modern civilization has lost so much strength and power. In fact, if it has still preserved some great qualities, it is only because the compulsive power of passion has not allowed itself to be completely smothered, and every now and then takes its revenge. Many writers and psychologists are of the opinion that the atonicity of the modern world is to a great extent due to its excessive rationalism. In my youth I read a novel, I believe by Heinrich Mann, in which all the children born of a prince's *mariage de convenance* were weak-minded, and were compared unfavorably with the child whom the prince had begotten out of his passion for a shepherdess: this child was a genius. The story obviously cannot be quoted as scientific evidence but nevertheless it bore witness to an indisputable truth: without passion man can do nothing.

If we consider ourselves, other people and all around us, with impartial and absolute objectivity we shall probably never succeed in making a choice which can commit our whole life; nor could we accept the challenges which such a choice would bring in its train. On the speculative plane serenity, objectivity and impartiality are precious values which must not be underestimated. But is it possible to achieve anything worthwhile by their means? It is possible when it is a question of deeds and words which do not immediately concern us. In a casual conversation I may of course speak quite objectively about the good or bad weather, but only on the assumption that my own plans are not affected thereby.

If I had already attained stoical indifference I should certainly be able to speak, think and even act objectively. But should I then have any longer the desire to act? In any case, existence, because of its own natural dynamic force, strains towards commitment, not indifference. As soon as we ourselves, or people connected with us, or activities or situations in which we are personally committed, are involved, neither impartiality nor objectivity is permissible, for they would lead to inertia and passivity. Whatever man's capacity for planning, his reasons for inaction are, from the rationalistic point of view, at least as numerous and compelling as his reasons for action. And since the danger of action is always greater than that of inaction the rational decision is bound to be in favor of immobility.

Innumerable people condemn themselves to inefficacy because they are, or wish to be, too clear-sighted, because they shun the illusions and disappointments which belong to all human actions. They get hurt by the contradictions and ambiguities of life. In their opinion life should be just as reasonable as a statement made in terms of abstract logic. But since it is impossible to banish all contradictions from our lives, these people give up all creative activity. We are not asked to attempt the impossible; we are not asked to banish all contradictions, but to overcome and transcend them. We have to integrate all contradictory elements in a higher synthesis, but this is only possible through a total commitment and surrender to something greater than ourselves and greater than all these contradictions. A young man may wish to give purpose and fulfillment to his life by serving a sublime cause. But he also discovers within himself the need for peace, for a safe and comfortable life. From a purely objective point of view it is hard to see what could influence him to make one decision rather than another. Only a burning passion for freedom, the brotherhood of all men or the glory of God, for art or some other great purpose can force him to a decision. Only passion can burn away all that is selfish and cramped in his desire for peace and comfort, and give him in a great commitment the more sublime peace of the soul.

Only a great and strong passion is able to endow his life with the breadth and generosity without which it cannot be creative. It will give him the power which will enable him to overcome all its pettiness and limitations and doubts. No obstacle can stop a man who is possessed by a great passion. Ancient and modern Christian writers have had much to say about the struggle that takes place in the human soul between reason and the passions. In their dramatic presentation they are perhaps inclined to dissect the unity of the human person rather too much. But we have no serious objections to attributing certain reactions and tendencies of our two-fold ego to reason, and others to passion.

Nevertheless, we are not at all in agreement with the assumption that reason is always right. According to its own nature it strives to procure the well-being of the individual, and does not consent to any sacrifice for the sake of ends which transcend personal advantage. If we had always been ruled by reason the human race would probably have vanished long ago from this earth! An example of this rationalistic attitude is seen in a certain policy for encouraging procreation, which sets out to appeal exclusively to the reason. However urgently a land may need its children, and however great the danger of the disappearance of any given race may be, the reasons adduced are in fact too remote and too impersonal to persuade married couples to bring numerous children into the world. Those who already have many children have begotten them for quite different reasons, for affective reasons. Moreover, we may add another example: it is much more reasonable to keep one's own money to oneself rather than give it to the poor, just as it is more reasonable to prefer one's own present and mediocre well-being to the dangers of the future.

It is quite wrong to separate reason from the emotions as if the former were the source of all good and the latter the source of all evil. In our opinion we have no reason to suppose that reason alone is God's gift, capable of leading us to salvation, and that the force of passion is the work of some evil spirit. In spite of being somewhat under the influence of Jansenism, Pascal himself admits that in the dispute between reason and passion the latter is not always in the wrong. Indeed, the great Christian thinker goes on to say, there is no true human greatness without passion. About the passion of love he says: It is through passion that we rise above ourselves and become generous. Passion breaks down the static equilibrium which the ego has set up, and breaks through the all too narrow framework in which reason wishes to imprison our lives.

*   *   *

It is not our intention to idolize the passions as if they were sources of greatness alone. We certainly do not ignore the devastation they have caused in the lives of individuals and societies. How many crimes and ruined lives, and how much misery have their origin in the ruthless outburst of some passion! The passions have dishonored many honorable people and turned loyal men into traitors and apostates. Would the revolutions of 1789 and 1917 have produced reigns of terror and dictatorships if the passions of hatred and revenge had not first invaded men's breasts? Many wars — such as Napoleon's and Hitler's — which have wrought so much havoc, had as their immediate cause the passionate craving for power of a man or of a party. It is beyond a doubt that a man who could succeed in excluding all passion from his life would spare himself great loss and suffering. The Stoics and the Buddhists make the annihilation of passion the aim of their spiritual endeavors, in order to find happiness in total indifference.

In the intellectual sphere we find the most numerous and the worst of the errors of philosophers and scientists, simply because they have set aside total objectivity and allowed themselves to be swayed by passion. For example, the passionate anti-clericalism of many biologists and philosophers (Sartre included) led them to most unjustified conclusions. The business of government would certainly be carried on better if politicians sought the good of the nation quite objectively and showed less party passion. We have therefore no illusions about the dangers and challenges which men are faced with when they give a loose rein to their passions.

Yet it does not seem to us that reason and the intellect, if left to themselves and to their own laws, serve order any better than passion. Certainly great advances in scientific, technical, philosophical and theological fields are the work of the intellect, which sheds more light on nature as it probes ever more deeply into the cosmic mystery. But it is by no means proven that all these discoveries and inventions have brought us any more happiness. For example, it is a historical fact that the condition of the proletariat, which caused such misery and aroused rebellion, was the immediate consequence of the scientific and technical discoveries of the eighteenth and nineteenth centuries. That modern wars are no longer restricted to killing soldiers, but that their victims are at least equally numerous among old people, women and children, is also to be attributed to the new conquests we owe to the slaves of the intellect. The end of Hiroshima illustrates the dreadfully destructive power of the intellect when it has cut loose from morality and love.

In the specifically spiritual sphere the devastation caused by the intellect is equally significant. Anyone carefully observant of our sick world today, has been forced to admit that, as Bergson said, it has lost its soul. No breath of the spirit quickens the numerous doctrines, world concepts and systems which have been put forward during the last two centuries. The spiritual death and the spreading of materialistic doctrines in nearly all social classes express what is called, generally without intentional irony, the intellectual life of this

evil let loose in human life by passion is of no account. Whether we speak of divine love, or love in marriage or friendship, or love for mankind, music or philosophy, it is creative only when it is passionate.

Undoubtedly every powerful passion runs the risk of being not creative but destructive. Instead of producing saints like Francis Xavier and Charles de Foucauld it may produce inhuman creatures like Hitler and Stalin. This danger must not, however, be taken as an excuse to reject great passions. According to Pascal it is better to repair the damage caused by the excess of passion rather than to try to eliminate it, for no passion can exist without some excess. The specific role of passion in our lives consists precisely in this, that it lifts us out of our natural limitations — and it cannot do this, as Pascal says, without some excess. Naturally it is not always easy to repair the harm caused by an outburst of passion. But we must realize that passion does not necessarily do harm: the harm is one of the possible consequences of the unavoidable dangers it brings in its train.

* * *

Because of ancient prejudice we often believe that illustrious people have let themselves be guided exclusively, or almost exclusively, by reason, and that the passions play an important part more commonly with inferior people. Experience teaches us that the contrary is true. Generally speaking the less spiritually mature people are led not so much by passions as by routine, custom, caprice or "rational" calculation. They experience only very mediocre passions — and are incapable of even so elementary an emotion as wrath. They are at most merely indignant or resentful. With them love is less like a passion than like the satisfaction of a merely animal instinct.

The more spiritual a man is and the more intensely he lives, the stronger are his passions. We quote once more

7

from Pascal, who had no illusions about the dangers of passion and yet asserted: "In a great soul all is great." The submen of the novels of Gide and Sartre are undoubtedly incapable of living with the same intensity as the heroes of Dostoyevsky. "An adventurous life," says Pascal, "is pleasant to great men, whereas the mediocre find no pleasure in it."

In our opinion a man who has never known a powerful passion is greatly to be pitied. We agree with Kierkegaard that "the man who has lost all in passionate love has lost less than the man who has never known it." However dreadful the consequences of a first loss may be, they are hardly ever irreparable. The possibility of conversion is always open to the victim of passion. Some of the greatest saints knew what it was, before their conversion, to lose themselves in and through passion: we remember the passionate follower of Christ, Saul-Paul, the passionate lovers Mary Magdalene and Augustine, the ambitious Ignatius of Loyola and Charles de Foucauld. Complacent and "respectable" mediocrity is the inevitable lot of the man who has never known passion, says Kierkegaard. Certainly the Martyrology contains no single case of a conversion from respectable mediocrity to holiness. Passionless men often make excellent administrators, patient students of science or philosophy and — in static societies in peaceful times, when government is merely a matter of administration — fairly good statesmen. But, as history shows, these passionless men are dismissed from office and replaced with men of a passionate nature as soon as it becomes necessary to create and invent. A Poincaré in France, a Chamberlain in England, were rightly respected as good statesmen as long as peace and prosperity prevailed, but they proved their incapacity as soon as the economic and international crisis came. On the other hand, men like Churchill and de Gaulle showed no outstanding statesmanlike qualities in times of peace and prosperity.

Is it possible to pronounce a moral judgment on passion? Here also judgment is impaired by rationalistic prejudice which insists that only a rational act can have moral value. We frequently hear even Christians protest that there was no merit in doing their duty, because they loved doing it. Or they say there is no merit in their love for their fellows because this love is spontaneous, that is, passionate. Passion makes duties which objectively are very difficult become subjectively easy. If the rational act alone were meritorious, that is, morally good, then it follows that all that man does with passion would be morally worthless.

Next we must notice that the great intellectual theologians of the Middle Ages were not prejudiced against passion. Thomas of Aquinas considered that to do good with passion was more worthwhile, from the moral point of view, than to do it for merely rational motives. The man who does good because he is inclined to do so by a passionate love for God or for his fellow men is worth more morally than another man who does it only, or chiefly, in order to win a reward in heaven. Passionate self-giving in an objectively good cause is more perfect than a purely rational act of generosity.

Even modern scientific psychologists must not assume that passion diminishes moral responsibility. If judges usually consider it a "mitigating circumstance" it is because they are implicitly rationalistic and believe that human passion is an instinctive and fatal power against which we can do nothing, or only very little. In reality, passion is just as spiritual — or capable of being spiritualized — as reason itself. Even if the unleashing of passion produces disaster and catastrophes, freedom itself will not thereby be abolished. At the moment when the passionate act takes place freedom is more or less shackled, but we have already shown that the freedom of no human act — even of a rational act — is ever absolute. It would indeed be more correct to speak about the commitment of freedom rather than of its shackles. As freedom is the source of passionate deeds, because man freely yields to his passions, just for this reason he cannot evade responsibility for any of his actions.

Here we have reached the heart of the problem. He can make a good or bad use of all his capacities and inclinations, and therefóre also of his passions. Relatively speaking and considering its nature, passion is neither worse nor better than the intellect, reason, the will, freedom, etc. If in practice it is the most dangerous of all — and we do not deny this — it is so especially because we have not yet learned to make the right use of it, and because the misconception that we are powerless against it is too widely diffused. In reality there is freedom in passion just as there is passion in freedom. It is our duty to become aware of the powerful affective capacity present within us. When we are aware of this we shall know how to put it to the best use in a true and generous life, and how to place our passions at the service of our personal vocation and God's work. The passions that have been directed to good ends no longer threaten to bring disorder and destruction into the life of the individual and into society. They may be compared to children who incur punishment for having done evil only because they have not been taught to do good. Therefore the training of passions should be undertaken as part of the general training of the emotions. There is no justification for stifling passion, for this would lead to the destruction of our power of creation.

* * *

In our praise of passion and of a passionate life no one must try to see proofs of our alleged anti-intellectualism. We do not set the emotions against the intellect and reason. Our intention is rather to oppose the Manichaean practice of dividing the human soul into separate halves, of which the one, the rational, is considered good and the other, the passionate, bad and perverse, as if the passions represented the devil's portion in man. The real man, as we have known him in our own psychic experience and in that of others, is an inseparable whole containing both rational and passionate capacities. Both reason and the passions are exposed in the same way to the danger of deviation, of preferring evil to good. The struggle between reason and passion is indeed attested by all psychological experience, but there is nothing fatal about it. As human existence is fundamentally dialectical, we cannot abolish these antitheses but we must try to integrate them in a new and more sublime synthesis. Passion must be enlightened by reason and reason must be warmed by passion. If reason enlightens our passions they will no longer make us act blindly and instinctively. Ambition will not seek merely the success of the individual but above all the glorification of God and the good of all men. The craving for power will have as its aim not merely the glorification of the egoistic self but the affirmation of man as God's representative in the world. Even wrath will place itself in the service of what is right and good, and set itself the task of driving the traders from the Temple precincts. There will be a similar transformation of all the other passions. Through them the dialectical progress of men and of all mankind will be accomplished.

The intellect is only truly human and creative when we are capable of thinking passionately. We have already spoken of the poverty of reason divorced from affectivity. It is above all the passionate thinkers and writers who have exerted the most profound influence on the history of mankind. Who could rightly estimate what modern man owes to St. Augustine, Pascal, Kierkegaard, Nietzsche and Dostoyevsky? Kant and other "coolly objective" thinkers and philosophers are today read only by specialists, but fifteen hundred years after the death of St. Augustine and four hundred years after the death of Pascal the *Confessions* and the *Thoughts* are still unalterably topical. They are read in all countries and in all languages, not as old documents but as writings which concern us all personally and from which we expect to derive something vital.

A passionate thought cannot leave us indifferent. It forces us to express an opinion about it. Frequently, especially with

Kierkegaard and Nietzsche, it lacks objectivity and impartiality; it astonishes and shocks us with its exaggerations and paradoxes. It grips the reader and tries to convince him by force. Kierkegaard shows himself well aware of this characteristic of his own way of thinking. He writes: "Whoever wishes to serve one Master only finds that exaggeration is unavoidable." Nietzche's books often made a Christian angry: he feels himself unjustly attacked. And yet I know several Christians who through reading his books became more aware of the demands of their faith. Passionate thinking leads to spiritual commitment. Only a passionate and committed thinker can make others give up their own ideas to follow his. In order to wish to follow another they must indeed perceive that this man truly believes what he says or writes. Jesus often taught the same doctrine as that of the Pharisees and teachers of Israel, he read out and commented upon the same Biblical texts and made use of the same popular imagery. But with him there was a tone of sincerity which was lacking in the others, and the people noticed this: "No man ever spoke like this man," they said. And they left their homes and their work to follow him.

* * *

The most decisive moment of our life is when we feel a great passion which takes possession of our whole being. It gives our life its true character and dignity and casts a dazzling light on all that had seemed obscure and enigmatic. The hesitations and waverings between conflicting tendencies are now over. We shall find the necessary strength and courage to make the fundamental choice and boldly commit ourselves. We shall feel no alarm when we encounter obstacles and difficulties; in fact we shall rejoice at facing and overcoming them. For we shall know that every victory increases and enhances the creative power which has been set in motion by passion. All the petty contrasts between reason and the emotions, freedom and determinism, are resolved by passion.

If Christianity were merely a system of dogmas and doctrines it would have produced no saints or martyrs. A passionate love for Christ is the only motive and the only explanation for the wonderful revelations of Christian holiness. The truly religious life demands man's personal and passionate yearning for God. Christians who distrust and reject religious enthusiasm because they have been taught that firm faith can only be grounded on reason, will never do anything really great for the glorification of God. They may indeed live in accordance with Christian morality and the laws and precepts of the Church, but they will not live the true life of faith, which could give unity to their personality. Religion will always be a heavy burden for them, unless it becomes a mere formality. The saints have lived their faith with ardor, although they too have not been able to feel it and express it uninterruptedly: it often remains hidden deep in their souls. From time to time they have felt its compulsive power and, with the help of the new strength given them by the power of their love of God in those moments full of grace, they determine to carry on their work even in periods of spiritual barrenness and desolation. No passion can burn uninterruptedly.

We may also often observe that it is just these passionate men who succumb least frequently to the capricious power of an infatuation. Both their freedom and their reason are inspired by passion and so they have at their disposal the necessary strength to withstand the attacks of mere infatuations which may disturb the passionate equilibrium of their lives. True passion indeed creates the mighty dynamic strength of a person whose energies are all controlled and directed by a lofty ideal. It is only dangerous if it devotes itself to too mean and mediocre an object.

CHAPTER XIII

THE CHALLENGES OF FAITH

Many people think that faith avoids all the challenges of life because it gives men such certainty as to make everything seem clear and safe. According to Nietzsche's concept, many "strong intellects" must condemn Christianity because it despoils life of all its dramatic interests. Others instead envy believers because, they think, they have no problems and feel no spiritual unrest.

As we have already frequently pointed out, life is full of challenge and suspense because man takes it upon himself to control his own ego and his own destiny, and holds himself responsible for the whole world. According to Nietzsche and many other theorists of religious "alienation," belief in God exists only because the simple-minded man has not the courage to see himself as he is. In certain exceptional and compulsive situations he has become aware that an immeasurable power and an infinite creative love dwell in his soul.

But he lacks the courage to take hold of his own greatness, with all its consequences. He attributes therefore to God, or to some gods, all that in his own nature is noble and unusual. Religion, Nietzsche believed, has debased the concept of humanity because it has considered greatness and truth to be superhuman qualities received through grace. He thinks that only submen can accept faith. The Gospel represents a sort of degradation and repudiation of the self because it preaches trust, innocence, patience, the love of one's fellow men, submission and obedience to God. Man must therefore, through an effort of his will, free his consciousness of the burdensome presence of God. In order that he may live he must boldly declare the "death of God." The Christian faith is the enemy of life because it preaches self-annihilation. It offers suffering men the promise of an eternal reward but strips his life of all greatness and drama. Because it preaches temperance and moderation it can only produce mediocre men and Nietzsche accuses it in particular of having ruined outstanding personalities like Pascal. Many intellectual leaders today care little whether Christianity and its dogmas are true or false. They reject it in the name of freedom and of the greatness which should characterize life. The most tolerant admit that faith is still of a certain purely scientific interest to historians, ethnologists and, above all, psychologists, but only as an explanation of certain pathological states of the human soul. On the plane of actual living, faith seems to them an entirely outmoded question without any relationship to our existence in time and space. Philosophers and men of letters who seek their inspiration in Heidegger and Sartre attempt to describe and explain life with all its immanent dynamism without the slightest reference to faith. In fact, they behave just as if it did not exist. Their concept of the world claims to be coherent and adequate to explain the whole of life and they assert that there is no need to debate whether God exists or not. According to them faith has already been proved useless.

Existentialists, Marxists and all the various followers of Nietzsche think faith in God is but a form of cowardice. Atheists and existentialists say that man does not dare to recognize and admit the absurdity of life. Marxists believe that faith is a way of escape for oppressed humanity that does not have the courage to revolt and build a socialist society. He is content to be consoled with the promise of the future coming of God's kingdom in which there will be no suffering and no injustice, and we need not struggle and fight to establish this kingdom for it will fall from heaven as a gift from God.

If religion were really as they suppose, it would be quite understandable that the man who enjoys life and is psychologically sound does not hesitate when he has to choose between faith or disbelief. For many of our contemporaries indeed the words "faith" and "religion" have no positive significance — in fact they could not even attribute a meaning to them. This is especially true of certain strata of the proletariat in big cities who, under the influence of Marxism, see in religion merely a form of spiritual alienation. Not so long ago the atheism of the European proletariat was violent and full of hatred. This is no longer so, probably because religion is less all-pervading and less powerful than it used to be. But many in the working classes are, in general, still convinced that the clergy are in the service of the ruling middle classes. As today their attitude is one more of indifference than of hate, the class conscious trades unionist—in order to conform socially and "please the women folk"—may occasionally perform some external religious acts, such as attending the baptism of his children, or a church wedding, some religious ceremonies or the funerals of relatives or friends.

Numerous intellectuals and "enlightened" bourgeois categorically reject the intrusion of faith in the ordinary business of their lives. Some reject it because a religious faith imposes rules for their moral behavior which they do not wish to recognize. But today the majority who reject faith do so in the name of loyalty to human greatness and dignity.

*　*　*

Some unbelievers may even at times envy the believers. They think it must be so pleasant to find in faith consolations and explanations which make the burden of life more bearable subjectively. In moments of dismay or dire need they may even be willing to believe, although they feel that this is impossible for them. To these unbelievers faith seems like an additional sense, just as some people have an ear for music or the gift of telepathy — not possessed by others. This occasional wistfulness does not prevent most people from feeling a certain superiority when they compare themselves with believers. For many people, however, faith no longer presents a problem. They feel no fundamental dislike for it but they do not see of what use it could be to them. No metaphysical curiosity disturbs them. It is true that faith plays no part in the lives of an increasing number of people and yet it has an extremely important mission to fulfill' in the life of mankind today. Experience shows that its role is much more important even than that of, for example, an economic factor. An attentive scrutiny of individual and social existence shows that its influence has never become useless or ineffective.

To be sure, we all know Christians who lead ambivalent lives such as we ourselves also probably lead. They believe in God, in the Incarnation, in original sin and other dogmas. They also obey, sometimes in a small minded and over scrupulous way, the commands and precepts of the Church, attend Mass, fast at the appointed times and so on. But they order their respectable family and vocational lives quite independently of their faith. At most they allow Christian morals to govern only their private conduct. If they aim at greater business efficiency or more ambitious goals they behave in exactly the same way as the unbelievers in their own milieu in the same circumstances. If they sometimes allow a little room for scruples in their choice of means this at once diminishes their efficiency.

These Christians may succeed in doing great things but it will be not because of their faith but quite independently of it, in fact, even in spite of it. Just because they know this sort of Christian, unbelievers can say that although faith may possibly be a fine thing in itself they see no connection between it and the actual lives of the people of our age. If a man believes in heaven it seems logical that he should accept the obligations which may guarantee his entry there, but the immediate human tasks, the choice of an occupation or a vocation, the conquest of freedom, the revolution of society, etc., can and must be effected according to other laws and precepts. Whether a man's political leanings are to be to the Left or to the Right, whether he believes in a free or a controlled economy, and whatever vocational activity he chooses, these are all temporal matters which have nothing to do with faith. The "Sunday Christians," to whom we have already referred, apparently share the same opinion although they do not dare to confess it. They also believe the Holy Trinity, the Incarnation and the Redemption to be heavenly truths, and they hope through their faith to merit eternal bliss, but in vain should we seek to learn from them the connection between their belief in transubstantiation and their vocational occupation, or between the communion of the saints and their political commitment. If they were the only sort of believers in the world the existential prophets of the absurdity of life and the realistic novelists would be right to describe existence without making any reference to religion. We have spoken particularly about such Christians in another of our books about "the unbelief of believers." [1]

It would, however, be wrong to disregard another category

1. **Psychoanalyse des modernen Atheismus**, Arena-Verlag, Würzburg, 1962.

of believers. Although apparently less numerous than the "Sunday Christians" we have just described, their number is certainly greater than that of the supermen among the atheists. It would be wrong to portray a communist as a drunkard crazed by misery, who expects from the inevitable disorder of a revolution a limitless opportunity for plunder. Similarly, if we were to consider a superficial hedonist as a typically representative unbeliever, it would be easy to maintain that disbelief can only create submen. But only the most eminent representatives of atheism can show us what a man can become without religion. Would it therefore be asking too much to observe the same principle when we try correctly to assess the existential value of faith? Too frequently an almost heroic atheist is compared with a spiteful, dreary bigot, or to a world-minded attendant at the Sunday midday Mass. This procedure leads to the conclusion that belief in God is by no means necessary for a superior existence; indeed, the unbeliever is seen to be preferable to the believer and therefore faith must be a hindrance to life. This comparison would, however, be valid only if all Christians were like these caricatures we have described. The mass of believers must be compared with the mass of unbelievers, and then the latter will in no way appear superior. The élite of the unbelievers must likewise be compared with the élite of the believers.

* * *

The perfect type of Christian believer is seen in the saints and above all in the source of all sanctity, Jesus of Nazareth. If we did not take into account his religious faith we could not understand the life and work of Jesus. His every word and parable, his teachings and his miracles, his acceptance of his Passion and his death on the Cross, are not the deeds of a man who certainly believes in God but could be understood equally well even if he had no faith. The truth is that all his words and deeds are inspired by his most pure belief in his heavenly Father. When he established the foundations of his master work, God's kingdom, he foresaw many generations of Christians and apostles who would complete the work. Nevertheless he was still ready to die for this kingdom because his sacrifice also was inspired by his faith.

Apart from obvious fundamental differences, this faith was shared by the saints. No one can doubt the extraordinary quality of lives like those of Francis of Assisi, John of the Cross, Charles de Foucauld and innumerable other men and women whom the Church sets before us as examples to follow. Even the most embittered enemies of Christianity are proud to compare those who have suffered for their own ideals with our Christian saints and martyrs. The communist poet Aragon made use of this comparison when he spoke of his comrades in the party who had died in the resistance movement against the Nazis. Many unbelievers, to give but one example, make no secret of their admiration for Francis of Assisi. Agnostic and atheistic writers have carefully studied the lives of the Christian mystics and compared John of the Cross, Teresa of Avila and Catherine of Siena and others with mystics of other religions, and have not hesitated to acknowledge the absolute superiority of the former group. The philosopher Henry Bergson, before he became a Christian, had the intelligence and sincerity to admit that all the Christian saints, martyrs and mystics were what they were only because of their belief in God and Christ, and that they owed to this faith their dynamic power and extraordinary greatness of soul. Faith is not something added to natural greatness: it is that which creates greatness. If one saint can be said to excel any other it is only because his faith is apparently greater and more sincere.

It may perhaps be objected that the saints are too lofty and extraordinary to serve as examples. We prefer to consider Christian believers who seems nearer to us and whom we meet in our daily lives. The life of this workman or that teacher or industrialist is sometimes such as can only be understood in the light of faith, and this is equally true of many simple peasants and mothers of families. Faith occupies not a certain place but a pre-eminent place in their lives. It inspires all their deeds and words, it is the principle by which they have chosen their fundamental commitment, and the main motive of their loyalty, frequently maintained against grave opposition. With true believers faith, far from being something external to their daily routine, illuminates their whole lives. This is not because it offers them consolations and certainties but because it plunges them into the depths of life's struggle. It convinces us that there is a God and that this short earthly existence is a preparation for another and more perfect life. But it also teaches us that eternal life is not merely a reward for temporal suffering but also the fulfillment of our earthly existence. The believer therefore sets about his human tasks with an enthusiasm and a zeal which are hardly imaginable to people who believe all needs and things are finite. We must not merely "practice" our faith: we must live it. Religious exercises in themselves are not dead rules, not formal, half magical gestures, but symbols and sources of life. Faith must not be understood as a system that can be learned by heart: it is not merely a matter of offering people the best moral code. A true believer is not a Christian as he might, for example, be a communist or a liberal or an existentialist, or a Kantian or Thomist philosopher, however firmly convinced an adherent of one or the other of these intellectual systems he may be. There is indeed a Christian doctrine which all Christians profess, and educated believers are in duty bound to study this doctrine and deepen their knowledge of it, but it is not the knowledge of doctrine that makes a man a Christian. Nor can his doctrinal preparation indicate the quality of his faith. There are in fact innumerable believing and practicing Christians whose religious knowledge is very meager. The well-informed and the ignorant are spiritually nourished by the same doctrine. It is not true — as some external observers suppose — that the mystics enshrine their most personal and inexpressible experiences in dogmas merely because they are accustomed to thinking in dogmatic formulas, or because they wish to show obedience to the Church. The testimonies of all who have described their mystical experiences agree in asserting that it is through these experiences that they have understood the content of the dogmas. This is also the conviction of every ordinary Christian who at one time or another has experienced the nearness of God.

When the young Christian worker is trying to evangelize his factory or district, it is his intention to communicate not the doctrine but the life of Christ. He has to convey a more or less clear notion of the mysteries of the Incarnation and Redemption. Christians of all classes and conditions who try to make human society more just and brotherly express in their own lives the indescribable mystery of the Holy Trinity. If God has indeed revealed to man the sublime mystery of his inmost nature, it is certainly not in order to satisfy his intellectual curiosity. As he is by his very nature created to become the image of God he must find in the dogma of the Trinity the perfect ideal of what human society must become. Just as the Divine Persons share all things, as the Fathers of the Church taught, so we men also must share with one another all we are and have.

We shall not become holy merely by observing the holiness of Christ and his saints. Contemplation, as it has been described by Plato, Plotinus and, under their influence, by many Christian writers also, presents a pure intellectual concept: it makes God an object for man to consider. He may find much joy in this, and even, as seems to have been the case with Plotinus, experience ecstasy, but all this has little in common with Christian perfection. Naturally we do not intend to belittle religious contemplation, which is absolutely necessary for the life of faith. Better and more profoundly than speculative knowledge it enables us to understand the living God. There has never been a holy or zealous believer who has not practiced meditation. If an old peasant woman, who had never had any religious schooling, has such a fine perception of religious truth that no arguments can confound her, it is because she knows how to meditate on God.

But life according to God's will consists more in the imitation of Jesus Christ than in contemplation, which is only truly Christian and capable of attaining its end when it leads to this imitation. The believer lives in the sight of God, as the Bible tells us Abraham, and other friends of the Lord lived. For the man who seeks to become Christlike God is no mere object of contemplation and religion no mere formality: he has an intimate personal relationship with God. Judas Iscariot must have meditated on Jesus and even admired him during the three years he spent in his company. If in spite of this he became a traitor it was not because he had contemplated Jesus too little, but because he had not tried to imitate him, had not wished to be as humble and selfless as he was. Moreover, the believer knows that he does not imitate Christ as if he were copying a mere image, men imitate a famous artist, poet or saint. To imitate Christ means working and fighting alongside him.

The existential philosophy of Sartre has declared war on the spirit of earnest endeavor. It all comes to the same thing, whether you get drunk alone or rule over many peoples, for all human endeavors will unavoidably and in like manner come to nought. On the contrary the believer can and must take life seriously. It is for him no vain and meaningless exercise to while away the time. Life seems to him a mighty task which is not confined to this world but reaches out to eternity. Since his life is committed to time, in which his eternity is to be fashioned, the believer dare not take life lightly, just as he dare not deal thoughtlessly with the life of the smallest creature. He is never justified in behaving like an actor "who," writes Albert Camus, "knows that at the end of his three hours' stint he will no longer be a king but who nevertheless plays his kingly part with due seriousness." Such seriousness has really no significance. The Christian's attitude to all other creatures must be like that of the priest at the altar. He knows that through him, through his daily activity, the whole world is consecrated to God. The sorrows and failures of life are for him no meaningless vexations, for he knows that they also contribute to God's great work: we know, with St. Paul, that all things work together for good for those who love God.

The believer must never be complacent, for complacency is closely akin to death. Belief is the principle of life and so refuses to submit to death. Because he is aware of his mission and task as God's collaborator the believer can be content with no given or contrived situation. The present must forever be overtaken by the new. The Christian, in a truer and greater sense than the Trotzkyist, is a "permanent revolutionary."

CHAPTER XIV

THE LAST CHALLENGE

Is our long description of the challenges of life to be finally nothing more than vain theorizing? Can nothing protect man, in spite of all his endeavors, from the dreadful reality of death? On that very day when he least thinks of it, when he is sure he has at last found his right road and can perfect the master work of his life, death will knock at his door and interrupt his plans and actions forever. Even if he dies of old age, in the evening of a long life full of satisfactions, death will seem equally dreadful. He has tried over many years and now at last succeeded in amassing wealth, wisdom and honors: all at once he must give up all these and go forth as poor and naked as on the day of his birth.

We must therefore understand the feeling of total bewilderment of those philosophers who pondered over man's life and came up against the inevitability of death. According to Martin Heidegger the best definition of man is "creatures born to die." He tries, however, to strip death of all that shocks us, saying that we must freely accept this life which ends in death and not consider this as a catastrophic end but simply as the last act. According to Sartre death is the end of life only in the eyes of others; only our "being for others" dies. André Malraux gives death pride of place in his work: it turns life into a doom and human freedom into a comedy, for all must end in death. As soon as man becomes aware of his own personality he realizes that he is mortal, and that consequently nothing has any meaning or purpose: death enfolds him like his destiny. "Man," writes Malraux, "is the only animal that knows it is mortal." And he describes in numerous novels the dreadful condition of this animal that is aware of its own mortality. All men are doomed to death and life is a torture chamber. The man condemned to death must bravely prepare himself for the final torture and try to cut a good figure on the scaffold. Sartre thinks along the same lines. For him the living are but the "unburied dead." Death is not only fearful; it also robs life of all seriousness and solemnity. All materialists and rationalists see more or less clearly that the reality and universality of death confute their optimism and humanitarianism. They hope to evade the problem by refusing to consider their own death or indeed the death of any individual. Only men in general, that is the worthless elements of an anonymous mass, die, but their place is soon taken by others and so all proceeds as before. It is obvious that a man will be unable personally to enjoy the fruits of his labors, but this does not matter because future generations will certainly enjoy them. According to this principle communists believe that they may rob mankind today of freedom and of elementary prosperity, in exchange for the promise that future generations will enjoy perfect freedom and the highest degree of prosperity.

* * *

If it were possible for a man to defer the awareness of death until the end of his own life, it would certainly exert a less decisive influence over him. He would then live and act according to his chosen ideals and when he saw the hour of death approaching he would try, like the Stoics, to die a fine death. Afterwards only other people would speak of his death and notice his absence. But we know that as soon as man awakens to consciousness of himself and to freedom he sees himself as mortal. The death of animals, the fall of leaves in the autumn, and above all the deaths of familiar and beloved people warn him that he too must only one day die. The sudden death of someone, which he himself witnessed or which he heard described, reveals to him the utter uncertainty of the duration of his own life, the possibility that he may die at any moment. Mentally alert children, even when only five or six years of age, often show a profound fear of dying. Gradually the awareness of death becomes ever more present and compulsive. Painful physical or moral partings from loved ones, illness and old age show themselves as partial experiences of death. It is indeed hard for thinking men to see life as directed towards anything but death.

If we see death from the immanentist[1] point of view it certainly seems to confirm the utter insignificance of human life. Existentialism, with its doctrine of absurdity and hopelessness, is undoubtedly the most logical philosophy derived from immanentism. It knows only the reality of every day, which is truly full of corruption, decay, death and slaughter. Many of our contemporaries live their daily lives according to this immanentist theory and therefore they see death in general as an insignificant occurrence, no more tragic than the death of animals or the fall of leaves. But they feel dreadfully afraid of their own death because they can see in it merely the annihilation of all their plans and undertakings. From their point of view all human activity must seem not a creative work but only a game which is important chiefly because it can prevent us from thinking about death.

---

1. For the immanentist the metaphysical absolute is no longer God, but nature (or man). Nature is divinized and is put in God's place. As a result, the immanentist seeks the explanation for all reality in the principles of nature itself.

Only from the religious point of view can we see death as something other than an absurdity and a final calamity. Just because we are mortal, existential faith is something more than just one of various spiritual factors: it is the condition for all true being. Malraux is right when he says that we are the only creatures that are aware of their own mortality, but our attitude to death must not be that of a condemned man. A man condemned to death usually makes no plans for a new house or for a marriage, and makes no further effort to improve his career. Even if he does not know the day and hour of his execution he sets about drawing up his last will and bidding farewell to his family. His life now belongs to the past. At most he can only hope to be able to forget his actual situation. If we were really sure of being condemned to death we should all behave like this man. We should be conscious of our future execution; only its hour would remain unknown.

Existential experience teaches us that men do not generally consider themselves doomed to die. They continue to plan and act with the serene certainty that they are achieving something positive, not merely for future generations but also for themselves. They study and acquire learning, sometimes even into old age. Would they do so if they had not the ontological certainty that death signifies no final end to their lives, no total destruction? There exist in men's souls some certainties more firm and profound than those of rational syllogisms. Would Heidegger and Sartre have built up their philosophical systems if they had not cherished the ontological hope that it is still worthwhile to wish to live? Neither the falling leaves nor the dying animals appeal to the "bar of history," yet none of us, not even the most convinced Marxist, would achieve anything if in the depths of his soul he were sure that death was a purely natural event. However bound up a man may be with his class, his race or mankind at large, he never quite relinquishes his consciousness of himself. History and it's judgment can only have a meaning if our death is not our end. One can perhaps understand that this ontological hope may be lacking in an absolutely selfish man, who may feel only an animal fear of death — but never in a man who lives and strives for greatness.

* * *

Although he believes in eternal life, even the Christian must not think of death as an unimportant occurrence. Like all thinking beings he also will feel anxiety before its mystery. He knows that it is the result and effect of sin and that just for this reason he may not consider it as of no significance. Even Redemption has not restored immortality. According to the warning of the apostle John, given in his mysterious *Revelation*, in the dramatic conflict between the forces of good and evil which creates the dialectic of life, death will not be conquered until the end of time. How can man therefore refrain from trembling before its unfathomable mystery?

But the believer sees nothing absurd in the fact that our life in time finds its end in death. He refuses to indulge in dissipations, in order to avoid the thought of death. He sees death as the best possible means of freeing the mind from everyday banalities and of giving life heightened intensity. Death alone is able to give even those who are most poorly equipped with natural gifts the chance to lift themselves above their mediocre existence and, in spite of all, to make something great and fine out of their lives. It is an old philosophical axiom that every action assumes its proper significance from its end; death is the end not only of one or other individual human action but of the whole of our temporal life and so it illuminates the meaning and purpose of all existence.

Let us suppose that, human life remaining as it is, there were no death to end it. Is it not clear that the great majority of people would be condemned to the most fearful tortures imaginable? To bear the burden of grief, illness and injustice incessantly and forever — everyday to begin once more the same monotonous labor — the horror of such a life is barely conceivable. For innumerable people death, in spite of the fear it arouses, is a longed for and welcome liberator.

Even if the immanentist and materialistic concepts were right, the horror of death would not be diminished. As the final end of life and the confirmation of the inevitable destruction of all that is human, death can appear to the conscious mind only as an invincible enemy. There is no theory that can stand the test of death. So long as man considers it only in a general sense he can well afford to play the hero, but as soon as he comes face to face with his own death or with that of someone he loves there is no more room for pretense or self-delusion. This fact explains the many late conversions, especially deathbed conversions, of people who have denied immortality with fanatical fervor, and we have no right to taunt them with their change of heart.

The believer tries not to flee from the reality of death, which he never doubts. It seems to him to be both the end and the fulfillment of life. It is the final and inevitable end of the empirical self, but it also helps us to realize that we are not this empirical self alone. It reveals that we do not belong only to this everyday world, but that we have something great and mysterious in our nature.

It is no mere coincidence that all civilizations, even the most primitive, have a cult of the dead. Even the rationalists, who are generally hostile to all "superstitions," think that death should be surrounded with special solemnity, and this is in itself a sort of new cult.

For the believer death is above all a transition, the passage from temporal to eternal life, from multiplicity to simplicity, from the transitory to the permanent. He unhesitatingly gives life priority over death. Temporal life is not to be considered as a preparation for death but as the testing ground for eternal life. This distinction is very important. In the former hypothesis all earthly life is a sort of gradual death — the less we share in its joys and fruits the better for us. But the point of view which we have adopted obliges us to live as intensely as possible. So that our life in time may resemble as closely as possible our life in eternity and may prepare us for it, we must make it as full and rich as we can. This does not mean refusing to make the sacrifices and renunciations which play such an important part in Christian spirituality, but these sacrifices must be offered not as a means of dying to this world but as a means of freeing ourselves and in our surroundings hinders us from living an truly human life. Not the transition itself but its purpose, not death but eternal life, is what matters. Yet, even from this point of view, there is always a mysterious solemnity about death which links time with eternity. Even the man who has failed in all his worldly undertakings may find a last consolation in the hope of death. The man who has achieved something significant in his life must also hope that death will in some way confirm his labors.

The Christian view of death offers us none of those superficial consolations which made Nietzsche think he was in duty bound to distrust and oppose Christianity. Although it is a passing from one life to another, death still inspires us with dread; even Christ could not contemplate it without some fear, because he saw it as the consequence of sin. It imposes the most painful separations, it tears us away from all that we love in this world. Certainly, we believe that these separations are but temporary, and that a far closer union is prepared for us all in eternity, but this thought does not make the parting less bitter. The tears which Jesus shed over the grave of his friend Lazarus surprise only those who have never sufficiently pondered on the mystery of death. In our attitude to it fear and hope are closely intermingled. We have an inescapable fear of having to leave everything behind, especially these bodies of ours which we think of as essential and inseparable elements of our personalities. Moreover, the believer knows that he is a sinner; even the greatest saint has not dared to think of his own death without remembering that it is the "wages of sin." No one can accept punishment blithely, and no one can think of himself as so righteous that he dare go before the eternal judge with unbowed head. It is true that Christians do not doubt Christ's final victory over sin and they know that death is but the passage to eternal life, but this certainty is purely objective: none of us can be absolutely sure about his own death, about its day or hour, or what awaits him personally after the passing. However unselfish we may be, it is impossible for us to think of our own deaths as being without special significance.

Nevertheless, this uncertainty about his own death does not lead the believer to despair, and does not paralyse him in the struggle of life. It causes him to feel an existential anxiety which prevents him from remaining content with the trivialities of our daily existence. Stronger than all fear is the hope, not grounded merely on desire but on God's promise, that he will live after death. In the life beyond death he hopes to discover the final meaning of life and to attain to its fulfillment. With men of strong faith this hope may be so intense as to leave no room for fear. In fact, there are many Christians who, like St. Paul, long to be set free, to be united with Christ. Ignatius of Antioch implored the Christians of Rome not to intercede with Trajan to prevent his going to the Lord. Many martyrs went to their death with joyful song on their lips, just as many simple Christians have accepted it trustfully, in peace and serenity.

But even to the most zealous believers death never seems of little importance. Although they may not feel fear, anxiety remains. They still tremble, not with fear of eventual punishment, for they have a great confidence in God's mercy, but with a reverent awe inspired by the awful majesty of death, and even more by the thought of the new life beyond. The apostle Paul, to whom was granted the extraordinary privilege of contemplating eternal bliss, admitted that the human tongue was incapable of describing its wonder. The experience of death is absolutely incommunicable — everyone must undergo it for himself. Although men have been dying for millions of years death is still an unknown quantity and it would be difficult not to tremble before its imminent approach. Even if we do not shudder with fear we tremble with awe as if we were awaiting some auspicious event which will cut across all the present contours of our life, and about which we can have no precise knowledge.

* * *

Plato was right when he said that the noblest purpose of philosophy is to prepare man for death. Unfortunately, however, we must admit that philosophy as such is incapable of fulfilling this function, and chiefly because all purely immanent philosophy has proved existentially sterile. For twenty-five centuries the philosophers of the West have tried in vain to fathom the mystery of death; the lights of philosophy are not bright enough to illuminate its true meaning. And philosophy is even less able to teach men how to die and, above all, how they can overcome death. In order that the life beyond death may triumph it is not enough to accept death bravely: it must be conquered. If no victory over death were possible, everything would be useless and failure and absurdity would be the final outcome, even if we could learn to die with the tragic nobility of classical heroes.

Quite certainly nature herself cannot overcome death. In the duel between them death would always win, even if science were to succeed in doubling the duration of life or even multiplying it tenfold. Only in spiritual and religious combat can death be conquered. If men, with their rationalistic prejudices, deny philosophers the right to beg from religion its necessary contribution of enlightenment, it will be impossible for philosophers to speak of death except in the manner adopted by the philosophers of absurdity, and this means closing their eyes to the mystery which surrounds it.

In itself death is a factor in the general decay, dissolution, corruption and ruin. Only Christ succeeded in conquering it and transforming it into a mystery of life and resurrection.

Since God's son became a man among men and resolved to share our mortal condition death is no longer seen as absolute and utter evil. Christ's death has freed us from subjection to a meaningless and hopeless doom; it has become a mysterious transformation, a passage from one life to another. Consequently it has lost its absolute character and become part of the general mystery of life, indeed one of its most decisive moments. It is no longer anything but an occurrence, but one of supreme significance.

Our attitude to death is as ambivalent as death itself. If death were only the consequence of sin, absolute evil, the end of life, then the revolt encouraged by Malraux would be the only conduct worthy of man. Malraux is fully aware that this revolt is inconclusive, and can remedy neither the absurdity of life nor that of death. It is just the same, he asserts, whether a man dies like a hero on the barricades or on the battlefield, like a coward in his bed, or as the result of some trivial accident. But the act of revolt enables men to escape from the consciousness of their own absurdity. Other immanentist thinkers recommend suicide. This does not save men from death but enables them to thwart its blind fatality and to decide freely on the hour and manner of their dying.

All these thinkers forget or ignore the fact that death is not merely the end of earthly life but also the transition to a life that is eternal. Resistance to death is resistance to God, to whom death leads. Since we can only reach perfection in union with God, a refusal to unite ourselves with him is a rejection of our final purpose as human beings. The uselessness of revolt is obvious because it can in no way save us from death. When we refuse to consider death as the passing from one life to another we turn it into our doom, into a passage from temporal to final death. The rejection of eternal life leads not to non-existence but to death, and the concept of hell truly signifies the endless continuation of all the pains of death, total destruction and the severance of our union with God.

Although the Christian believer does not rebel against the thought of death he is nevertheless not prepared to submit to its fearful power. He does not wish to live on this earth as if he were already dead, or condemned to death. To resign himself to evil would mean that he believed it to be almighty and invincible. But he knows that all evil was conquered long ago by Christ. To be resigned to death would mean submitting to its power, and that would be a denial of our redemption. The Christian's attitude to death must be neither one of revolt nor one of resignation, but the attitude of a warrior. Life must not be changed into death; death must be called into the service of life. The martyrs of whom we have spoken, who went joyfully to their death, which was often extremely painful, were not seekers after death. They were all passionately alive. They felt no scorn for life and if they accepted death so joyfully it was because they saw in it the surest means of winning through to eternal life. Because Christ, when he died in time, had conquered death, they knew they had to follow the same road. The desire to be as close as possible to their Lord was the reason for their desire to suffer a death similar to his. We cannot help being profoundly impressed by the extraordinary dignity with which St. Polycarp, for example, accepted his martyrdom, showing not a trace of disgust for life or of the Stoic's scorn of death. He climbed on to his funeral pyre as if he were setting out upon a long journey, the way unknown, but the end bathed in light.

The Christian believer is moreover aware that death is no private affair of his own but of concern to all his fellow men and to all who work for God's kingdom. His attitude to his own passing influences to some extent the passing of all others. It is his duty to resist death heroically, not as a desperate man but under the banners of hope and the promise of eternal life. He feels resigned neither to his own death nor to the final disappearance of the least living creature. If it were not possible to overcome death for all that live, there would be no justification for this world and we should still have to rebel against it, even if we were not absolutely assure of an eternal life.

Death is the consequence of hatred and sin, and so can only be overcome by love. We must passionately love all that lives, our own life and that of others. Naturally it is not merely, or even principally, a question of physical life. Without scorning this we must always regard it with a certain detachment. The victory of death over eternal life can only be the result of an excessive attachment to empirical life, which produces cowardice, treachery and narrow-minded conservativism. The love of life must mean above all the love of the spiritual life. The Christian must fight against his instinctive fear of the dissolution of his empirical self, and transform this fear into holy awe before the mystery of death; with this awe upon him he will meet God.

Must we therefore regard preparation for death as unnecessary and banish it from our spiritual life? On the contrary. We must banish only that kind of preparation for death which leads to the diminishment of the intensity of our living. However good the intention may be of those who make such a preparation, in the end it always serves the cause of death rather than the cause of life. The best, in fact the only good, preparation for death consists in living as intensively as possible on this earth, so that already in our earthly lives we may strive for the abolition of the barriers between time and eternity. The more truly we live our earthly lives the less fearful will appear the passage to eternity.

It is utterly un-Christian to treat the dead as if they were poor, unhappy folk to be pitied. Because of our Christian faith and hope we must think of them as living people, and our relations with them must be those of the living with the living. On the other hand, since we know that we are all mortal, it would not be right to treat ourselves and others as if we would never die.